I0756072

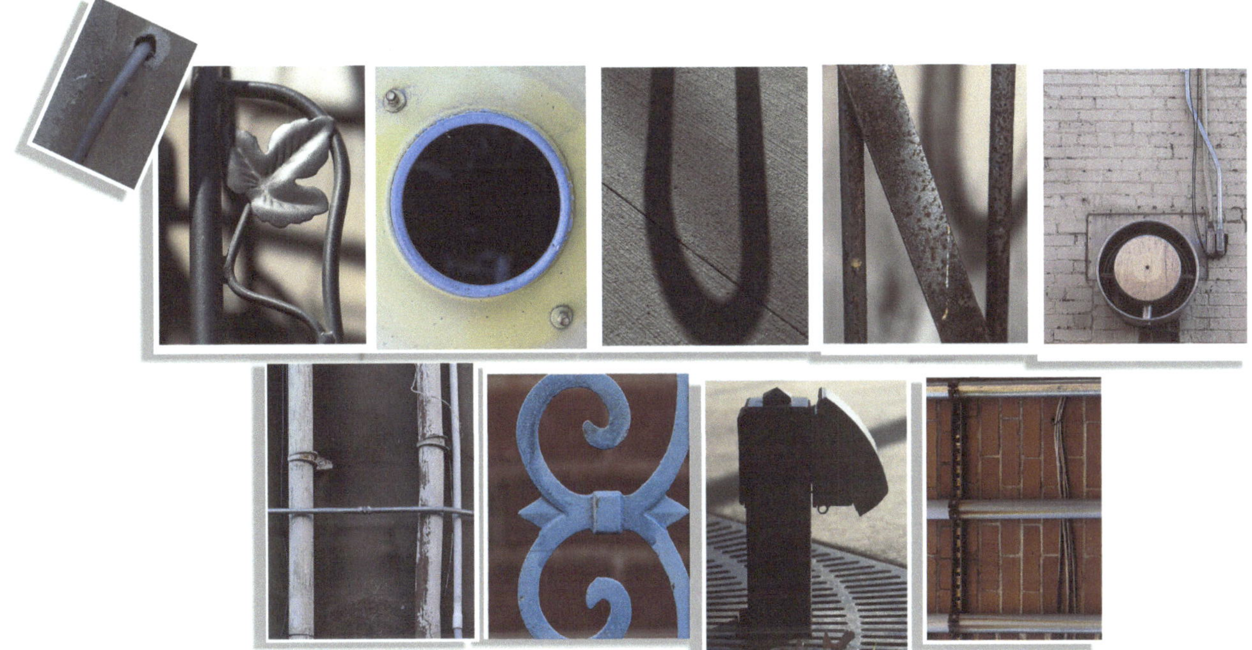

Also by Clayton Joe Young and Scott Owens

Country Roads: Travels through Rural North Carolina

Also by Clayton Joe Young

First Season (with Tim Peeler)

West of Mercy (with Tim Peeler)

The Birdhouse (with Tim Peeler)

We See What We Want to See (with Tim Peeler and Kelly Carroll)

The Last of the Young Men

A Celebration of Heritage

Mountain Folk

Keeping Our Traditions

North Carolina Places and Things

Also by Scott Owens

All In (with Pris Campbell)

Prepositional

Worlds Enough: Poems for Children (with Missy Cleveland)

Sky Full of Stars and Dreaming

Counting the Ways

Down to Sleep

Thinking about the Next Big Bang in the Galaxy at the Edge of Town

To

Eye of the Beholder

Shadows Trail Them Home (with Pris Campbell)

For One Who Knows How to Own Land

Something Knows the Moment

The Nature of Attraction (with Pris Campbell)

Paternity

The Fractured World

Book of Days

Deceptively Like a Sound

The Persistence of Faith

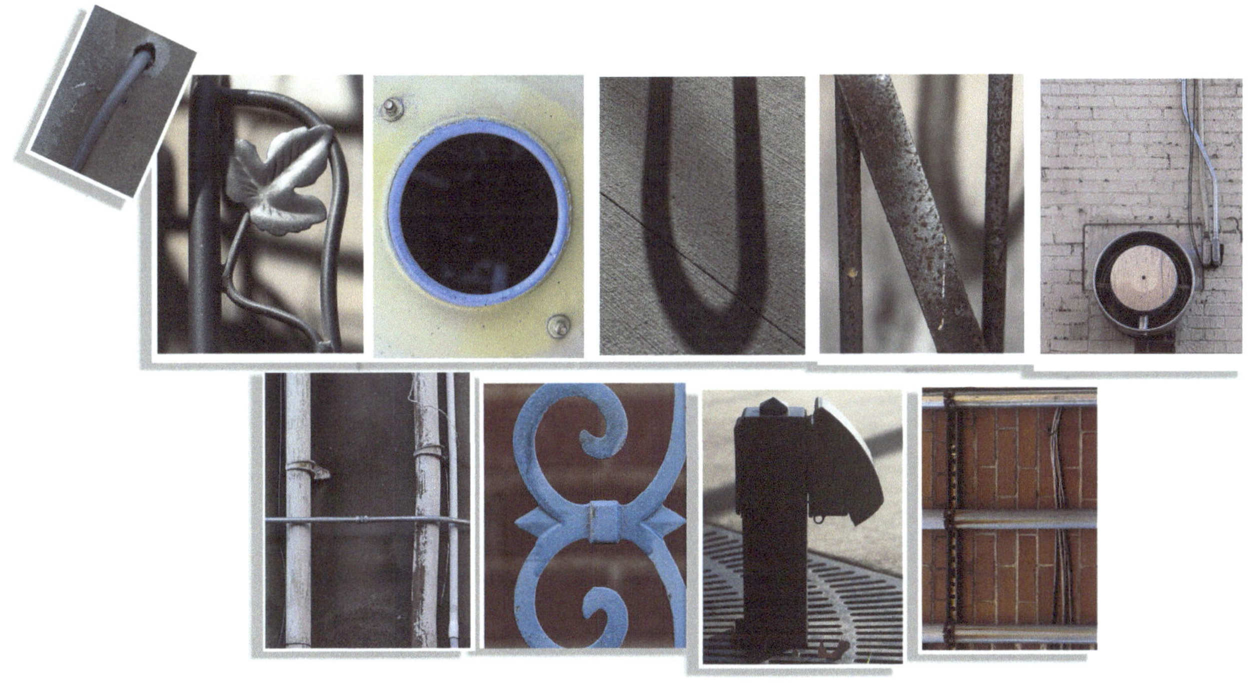

IMAGES FROM AND NEAR CATAWBA COUNTY

Poems by Scott Owens
Photos by Clayton Joe Young

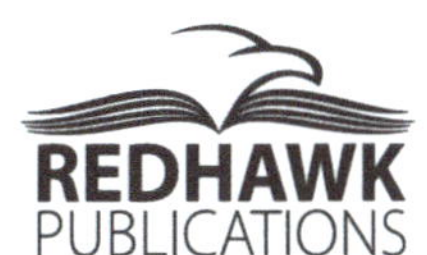

ISBN: 978-1-959346-23-4

Library of Congress Control Number: 2023947277

Redhawk Publications

Catawba Valley Community College Press
2550 Hwy 70 SE
Hickory NC 28602

https://redhawkpublications.com

Creative Layout and Design by Melanie Johnson Zimmermann

Printed in the United States of America

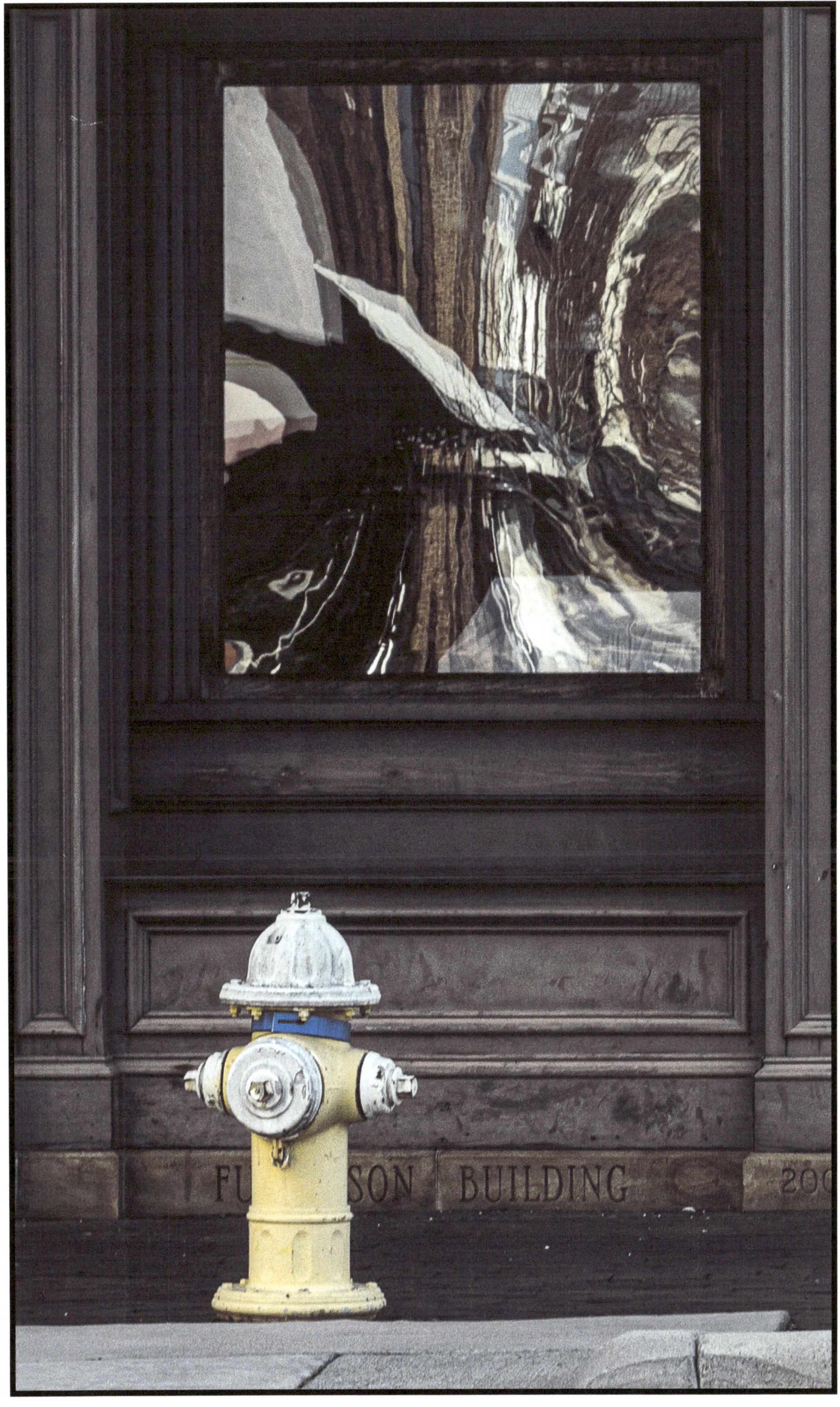
BUILDING

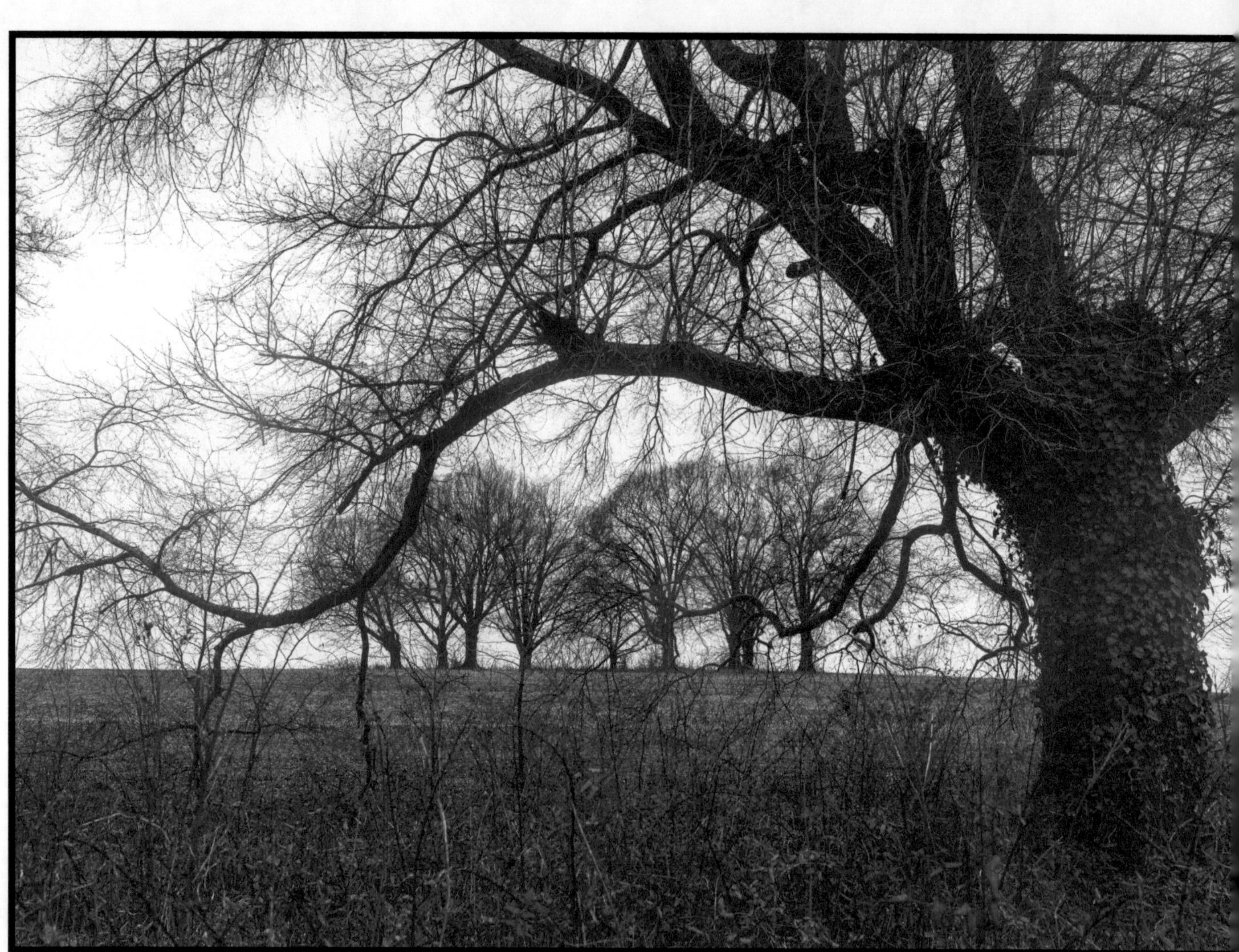

Used To

Murray's Mill
(Catawba County, NC)

Framed not through a window
but an open doorway as any view
of the past should be, inviting
the viewer to step through,
even if only a moment,
even if only in memory,
to what it must have been like
some hundred years ago,
same placid pond spilling
over stone dam, same waterwheel
catching what is needed,
same white wood mill,
same Dutch barn in the background,
on the same hill, with the same
reflection of trees as the same sun
sets in the west, in, of course,
the same eternal sky.

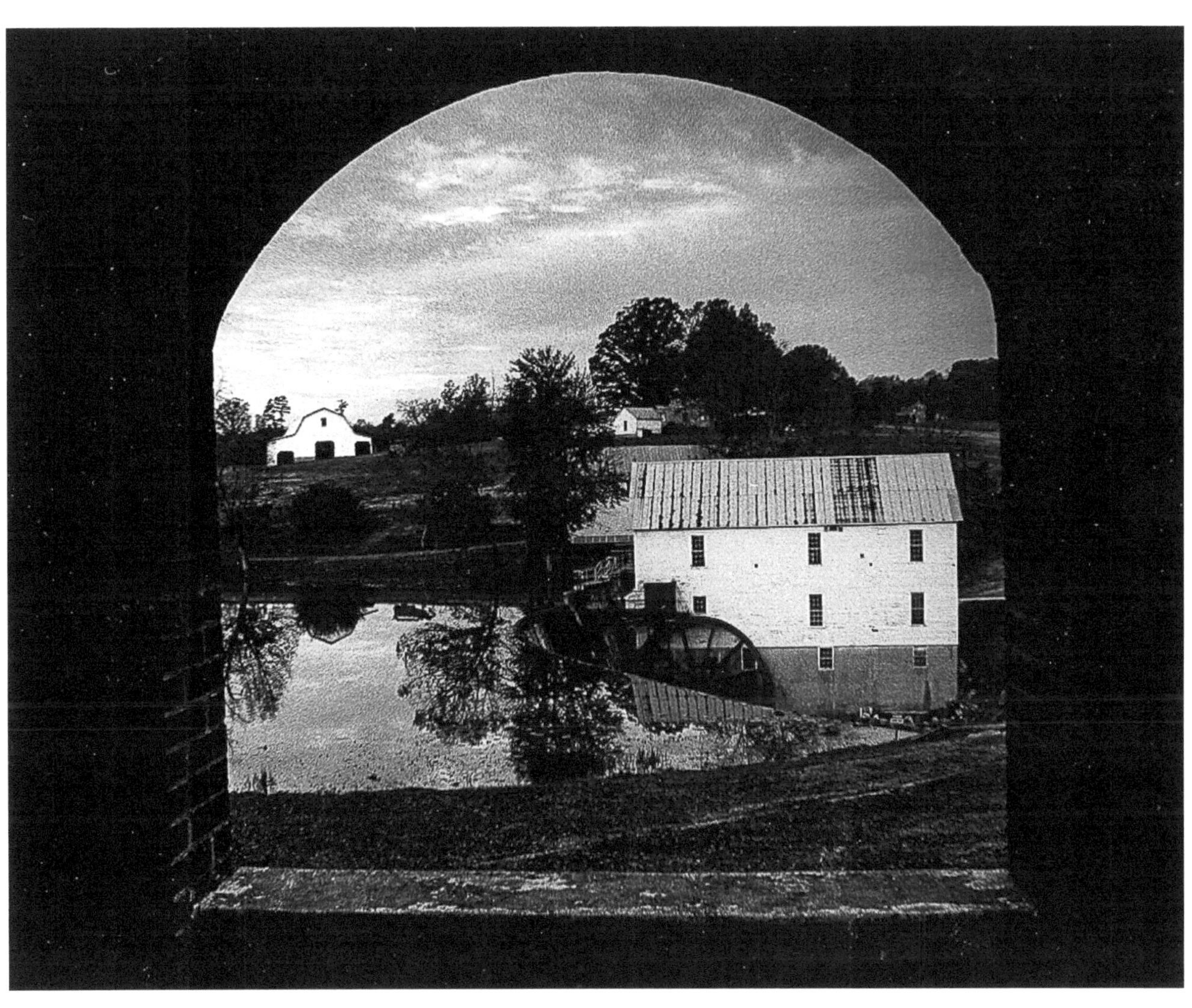

On Settlemyre Bridge
(Catawba County, NC)

On Settlemyre Bridge a boy drops a line
into water running below, the silver sides
of fish flashing as they surf eddies
standing still behind rocks as old as time.

On Settlemyre Bridge, beyond the shade
of ancient trees, a girl leans into a boy's arms
and laughs a little laugh at almost anything
he says, her face too bright to ever fade.

On Settlemyre Bridge the sun casts autumn light
through trees barely bare, littering the ground
with rustling shapes of the past year, expanding
the sky and bringing forgotten visions to sight.

On Settlemyre Bridge the land fans out
to either side, rising quickly to hills
decked with houses old and new, weathered
walls testimony to constant conquest of doubt.

On Settlemyre Bridge only the names change.
Another boy, casting bait, dreams
of water running to places he's never seen
and stands where time stands still and nothing seems out of range.

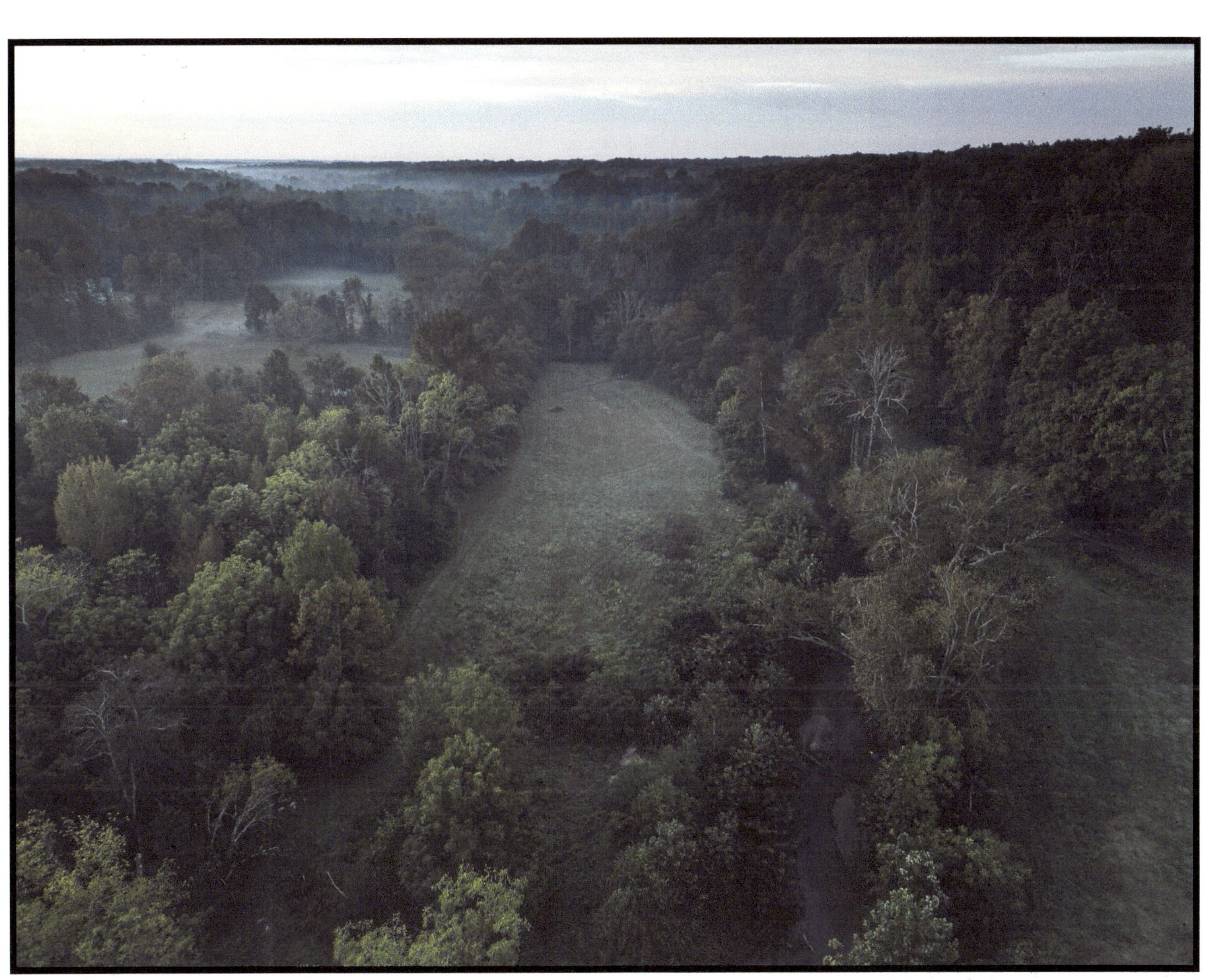

Mill Village
(Burke County, NC)

Rounding the curve
on Henry River Road,
they come into view
tucked beneath a canopy of trees,
house after house
descending the hill,
each one just like
the one before,
white clapboard, tin roof,
screen door slapping
against wood frame,
chimney the only brick
in sight except for one,
two-story, Juliet balcony,
looking out towards Baker's Mountain.
You know right away
entire families lived here,
Aderholts and Rabys,
Burnses and Rudisills.
You even think you hear them,
catch glimpses of young ones
running through backyards,
old ones watching from windows.
The truth is they left slowly
after the mill closed,
next generations wandering away
to find something more to do,
some way to sustain themselves,
the very remoteness of the place
leading to properties not
built over or plowed under,
but left standing
almost as if expecting
the people to return,
almost as if in memorial
to another time,
another way of life.

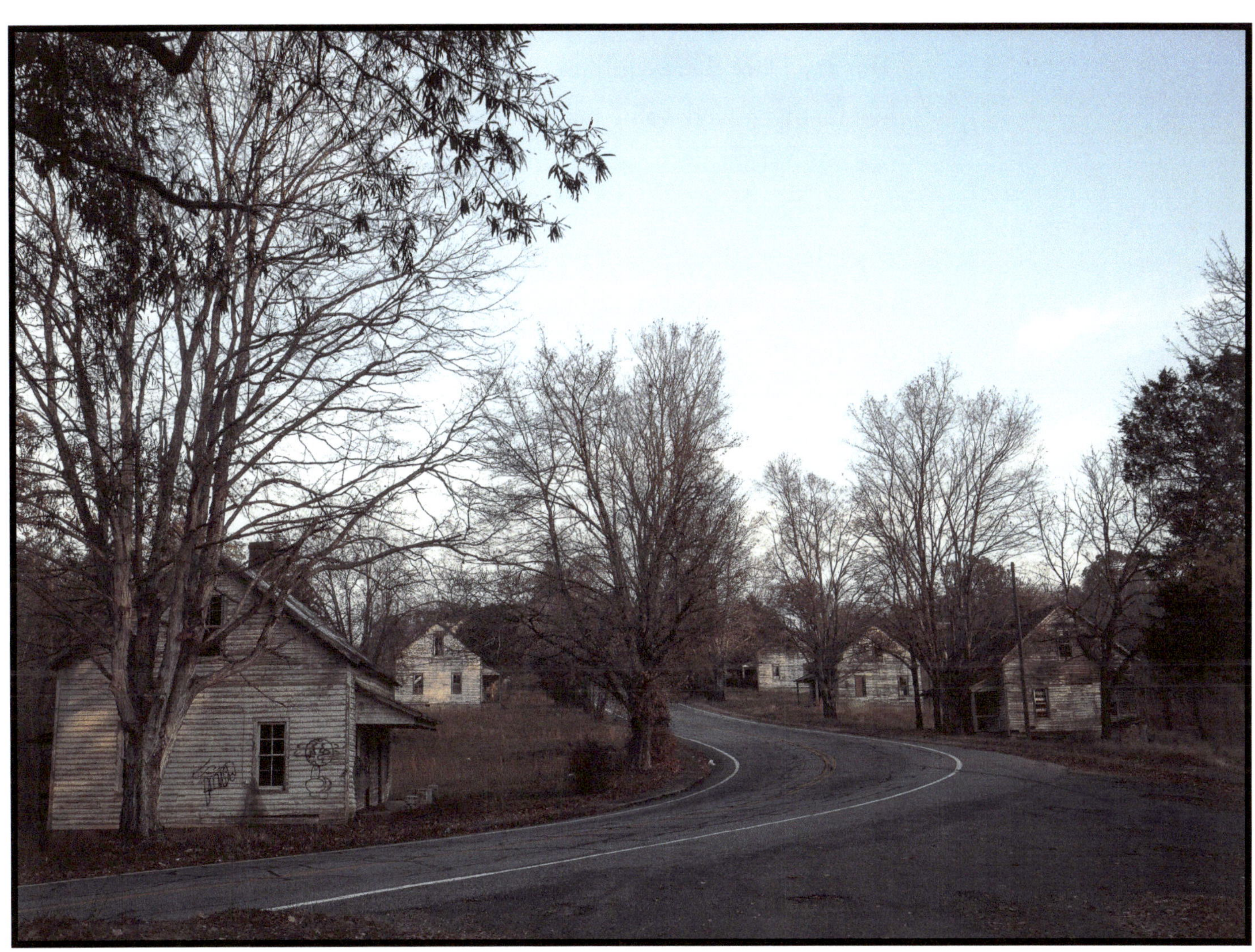

Cabins in the Woods
after Bob Hart
(Catawba County, NC)

This is a place there could be a village,
he must have said, so he made one,
not out of Lincoln Logs, Erector Sets,
Legos, the boxes and sticks we used
when I was 10 and 11, to make a town,
breaking off chunks of asphalt from the highway,
melting them over an oil drum fire,
pouring the viscous liquid to harden
into our own streets for Matchbox cars.
Rather, life-sized, real, more than a hundred
two-hundred-year-old buildings,
homes, sheds, barns, workshops,
churches, moved log by log
from all around North Carolina
and repaired, rebuilt, re-placed
around his pond, in the woods,
even furnished with salvaged
beds, tables, tools, each one
an artifact in its own right,
making a village not to live in
but to see, visit, walk through,
remember how it used to be.

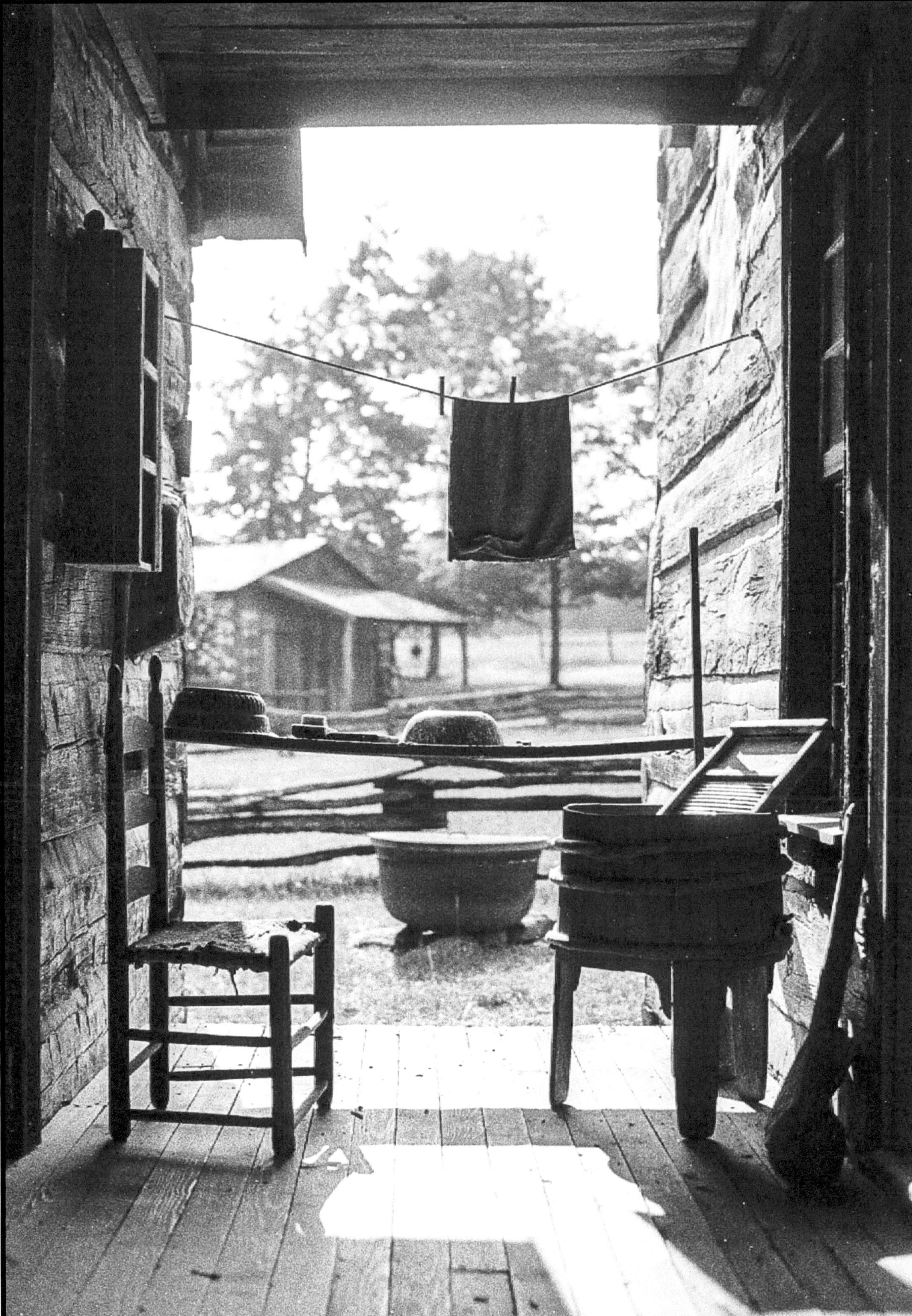

Seen Through a Glass
(Catawba County, NC)

Who can tell what is real,
and what is mere reflection?
The lamp, the window,
the world beyond,
or the world held captive within.
Blurred lines abound
in images that only seem
to coalesce, like memory
changing over time
given new perspectives,
new understandings, new
details that enter in
even when things are done.
Everything distorts, thought,
belief, attention, illumination,
limitations of sight, knowledge,
understanding, focus, periphery, depth.
Perception becomes the snow globe
we live within, the glass
sometimes closer, sometimes thinner,
but always curving around us.

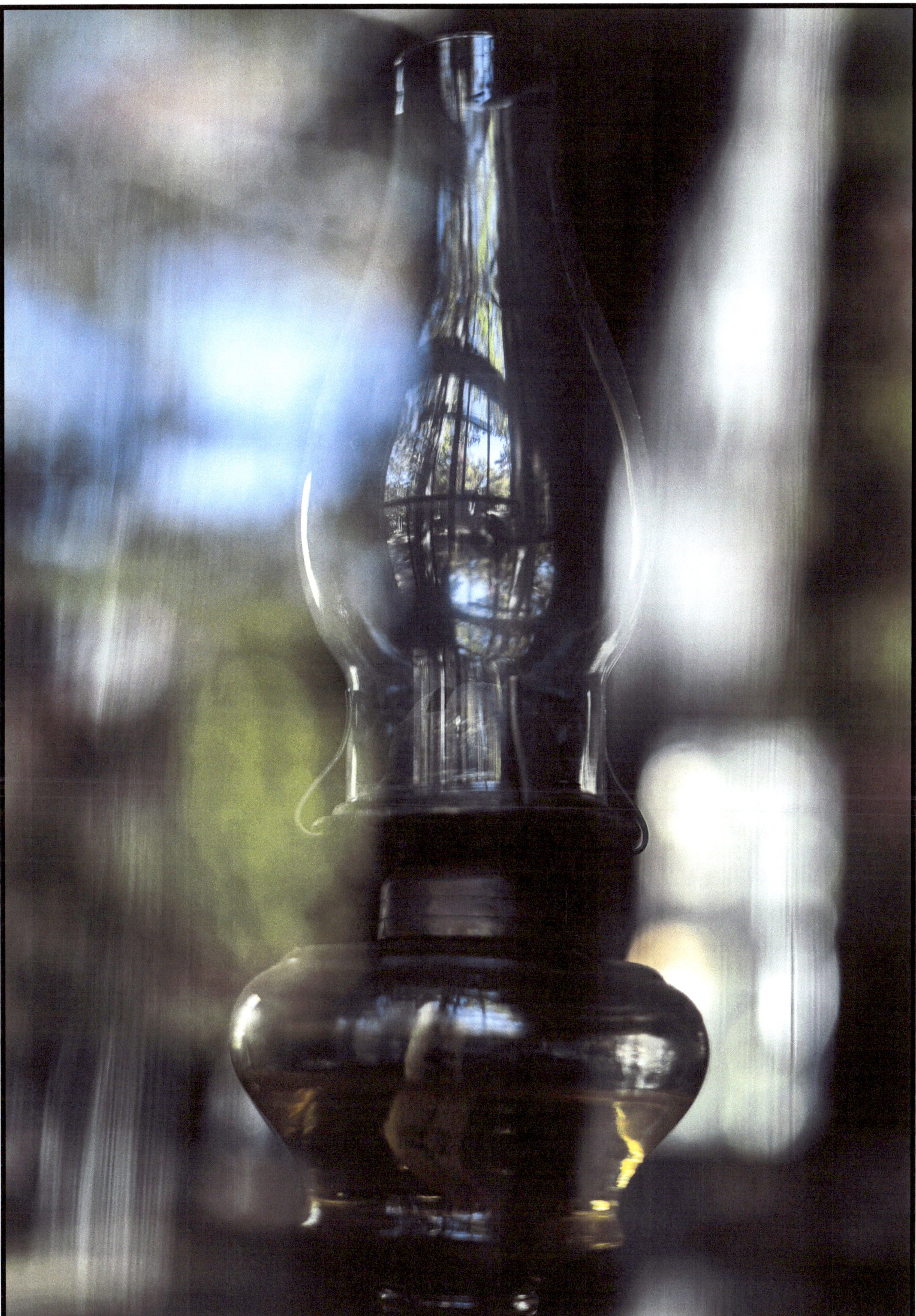

Equity
(Iredell County, NC)

Most of us knew nothing like this,
saw the insides of only ramshackle,
tumbledown, stitched together,
cabin, cottage, mere extensions
of hill, earth, stone, rising humbly
out of as if almost a part of.

We dreamed the country manor
such places implied, everything
provided, clean, and constantly full.
No chores, no mornings before dawn,
no smell of animals even inside,
no mud staining the floor.

Still, even then we knew enough
to know that even a house
this big was nothing against the enormity
of sky, time, place, circumstance,
that even a house this big
would eventually fall.

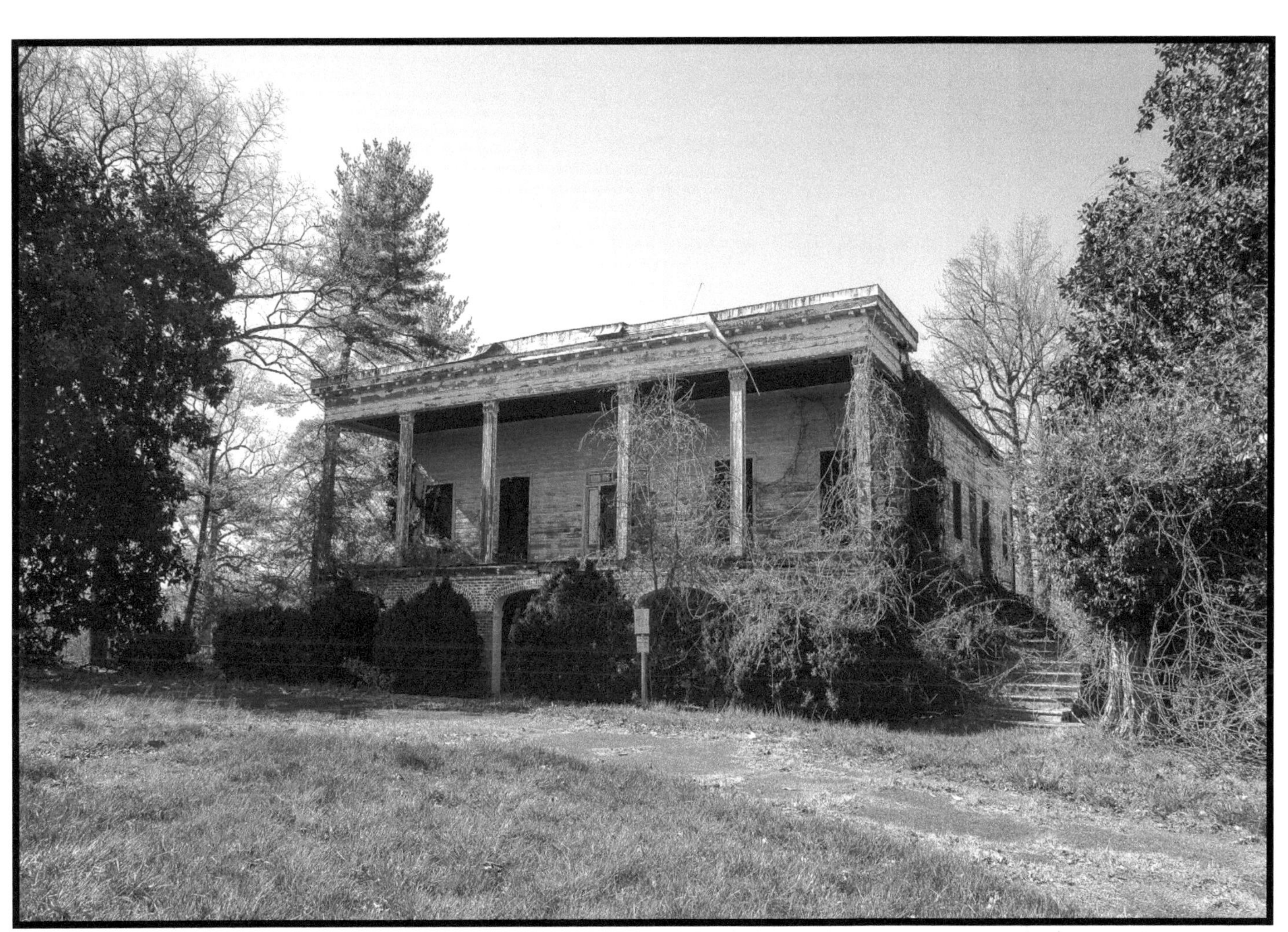

Open House
(Lincoln County, NC)

Where do the ghosts go when the walls
fall down, when the house that held them
no longer holds its own apart?

Where fly the eyes of windows
when panes are broken out, when frames
collapse like crosses heaped on the ground?

Where do skeletons conceal themselves
when closets are left with no door
to close, rags hung out in wind and rain.

Each year we return to see what remains.
Roof sagging, chimney falling into itself,
mimosa growing through floorboards.

A house without a wall is an open book,
each page whispering its secrets away,
a window the size of all who lived within it.

A house without a wall is a space
there could be a door, a threshold,
a staircase leading to something more.

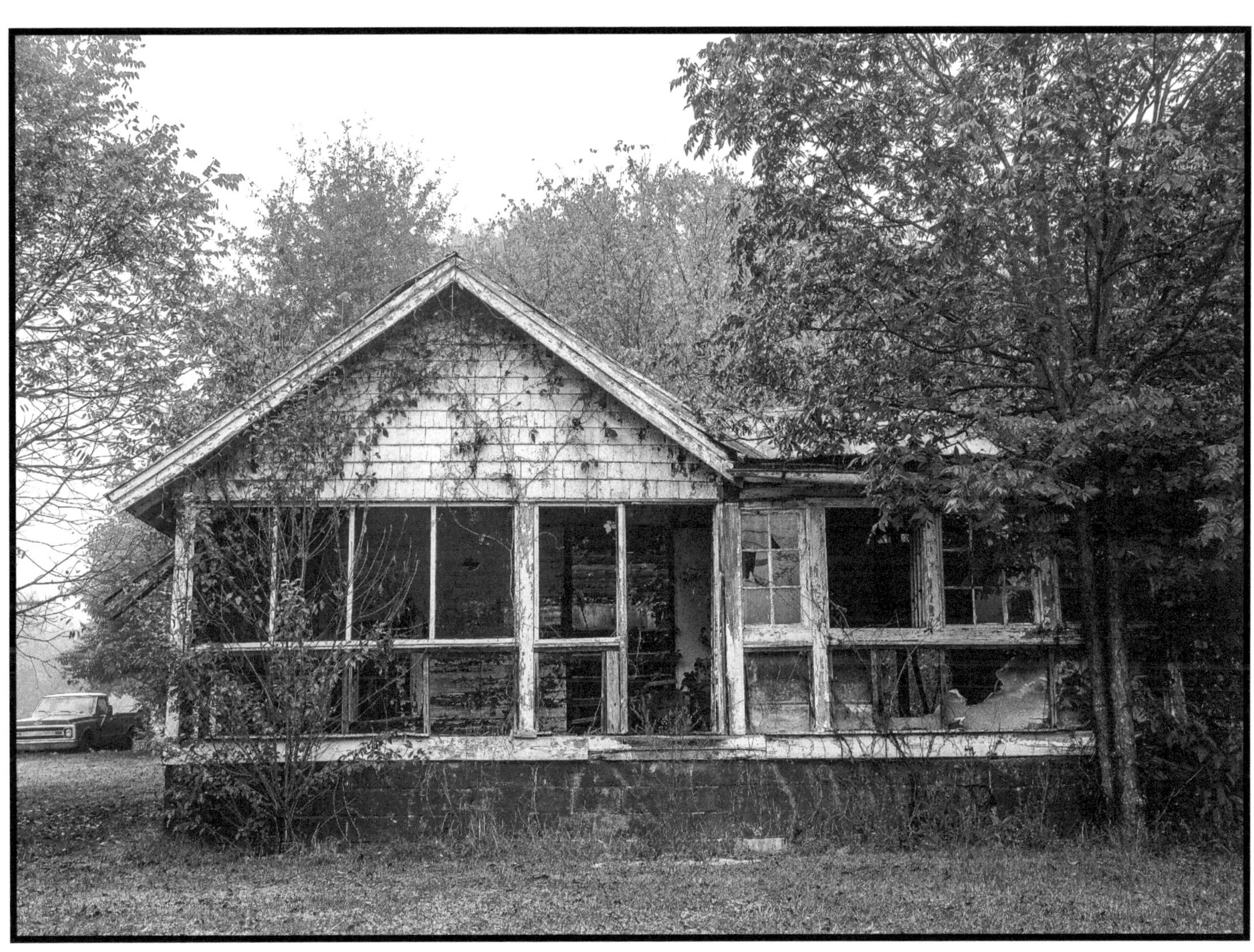

Ridgeview
(Catawba County, NC)

Dust Bowl, not the time,
but a place, and not a place
anyone would think history
would be made, not this kind
of history, not in 1964.
Sandlot dirt track, most of the time,
mudpit after rains, silent
witness, silent testament still,
to a kind of history none
would have thought possible
in a place this small.
An undefeated, unscored on
high school football team,
a group of boys, really,
black boys at a black school,
barely big enough to field
both sides of a team,
calling themselves Panthers
when the word panther
struck fear in the hearts of some.
Just boys like Allen Burch,
and Allen Pope, Lee Bumgarner
and John Hodge, Xenephone Lutz
and Tillis Rendleman, bound together
by a common cause, a common quest,
a common belief in each other,
and a coach who had nearly been there before.
When the dust settled, the final record
was 12 and 0, the final score,
four hundred and forty six to nothing.

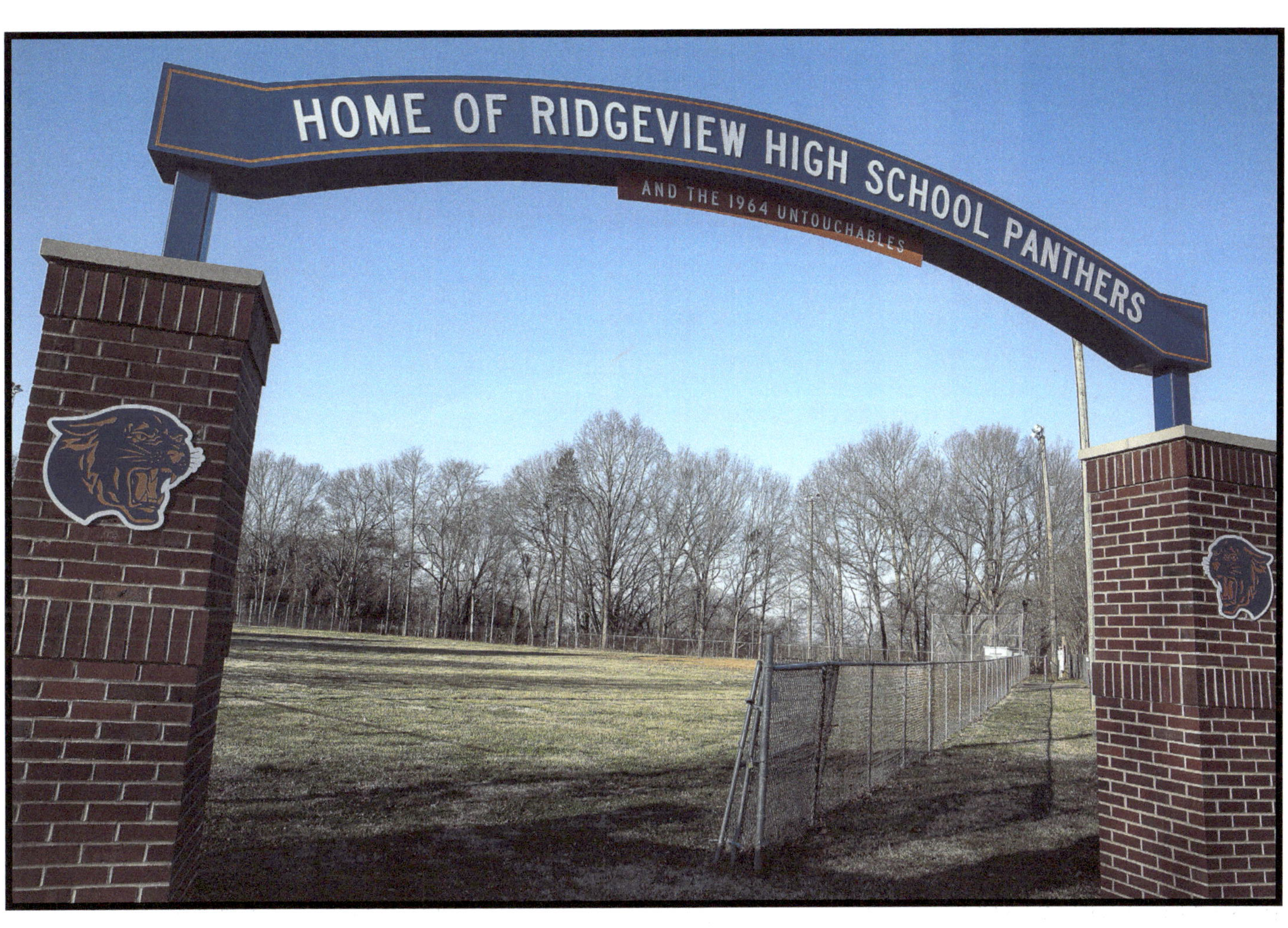
HOME OF RIDGEVIEW HIGH SCHOOL PANTHERS
AND THE 1964 UNTOUCHABLES

Connections
(Catawba County, NC)

If river could ever be said to be the same,
then this is the same river and the same spot
Catawbans crossed 6000 years ago,
the same that Colonel Charles McDowell led
500 British captives from Cowpens
across on their way to prison in Virginia,
the same that Andy Ramsour built a bridge
over in 1895 using the lattice truss
invented by Civil War general Herman Haupt
to save money, save iron, save weight.

Lyle Creek, fed by Mull Creek
and Baker's, Herman Branch and others
not even given a name, crossed here
at Bunker Hill Farm by Island Ford Road
on a covered bridge, under 100 feet
of tin roof, mostly connecting
wood and field at a convenient place
between where people come from
and where they want to go.

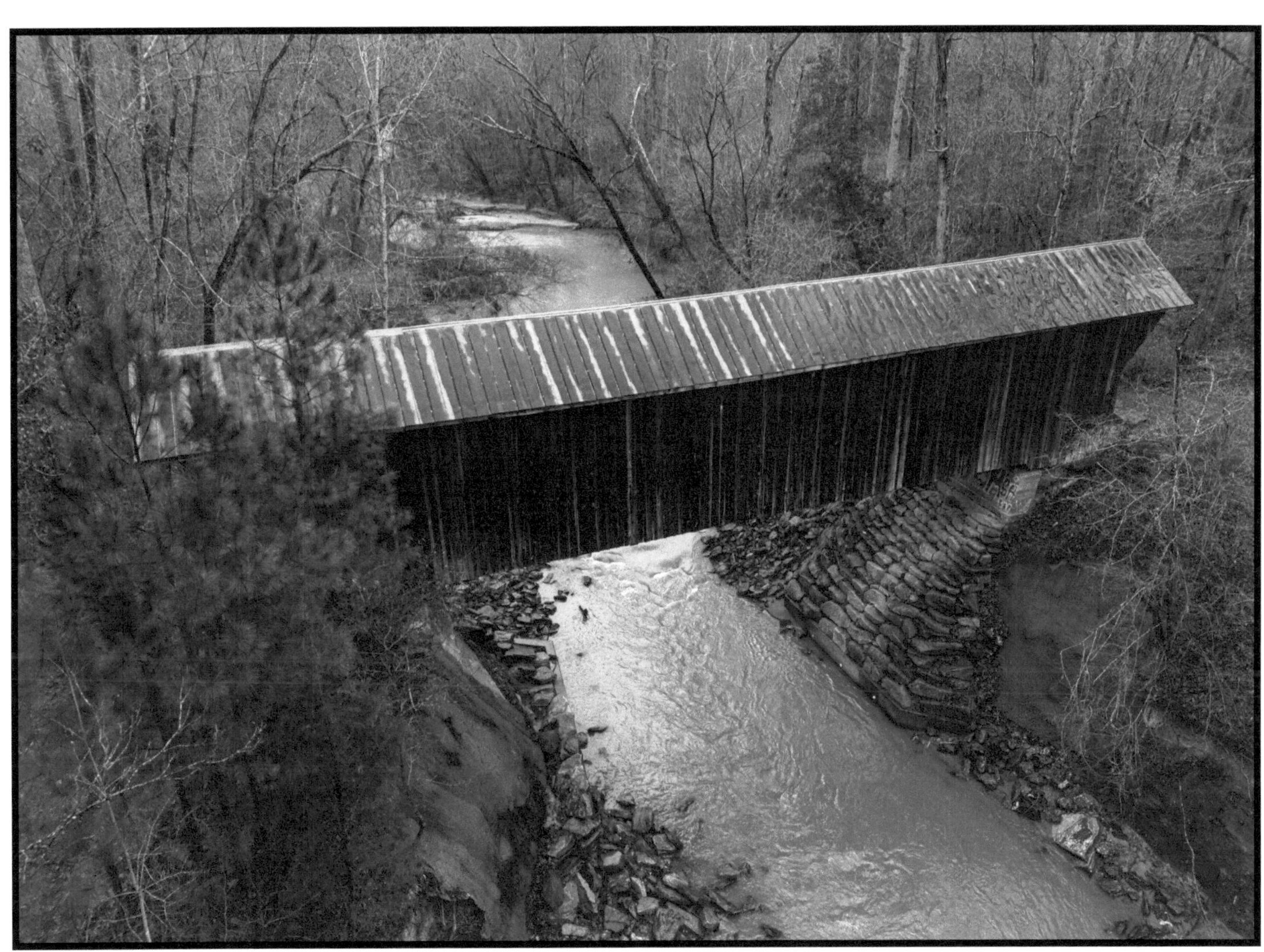

From Here
(Catawba County, NC)

No matter which way you look,
from Bolick's Dry Ridge
what you see is history:
Claremont High School's terra cotta details
and coffered ceilings preserved
in science, arts, literature together;
the Harris Arcade with the outside
brought in on broken tile terrazzo floor;
Romanesque granite of First Presbyterian Church;
endless windows of the Lyerly Mill;
the Carolina Theater's classic revival design
beneath Bacchus' watchful eye;
an idea repeated in City Hall, Fire Department
and Jail become Community Theater;
in the Elliot-Carnegie Library,
and the 1914 Post Office.
And if you look a bit further
you see the range of Hickory's homes:
Clement Geitner's double pile brick
on a stone foundation;
the Harper House, all gables and dormers,
tower and pitched roof,
Queen Anne indulgence preserved
in stained glass and brass,
parquet, wainscoting, and silhouettes;
Maple Grove's three-bay, two story porch
with four pairs of supporting pillars;
and the Propst House, an Empire style
doll house with mansard roof and tower,
all saved in a place that thinks
the past has plenty worth preserving.

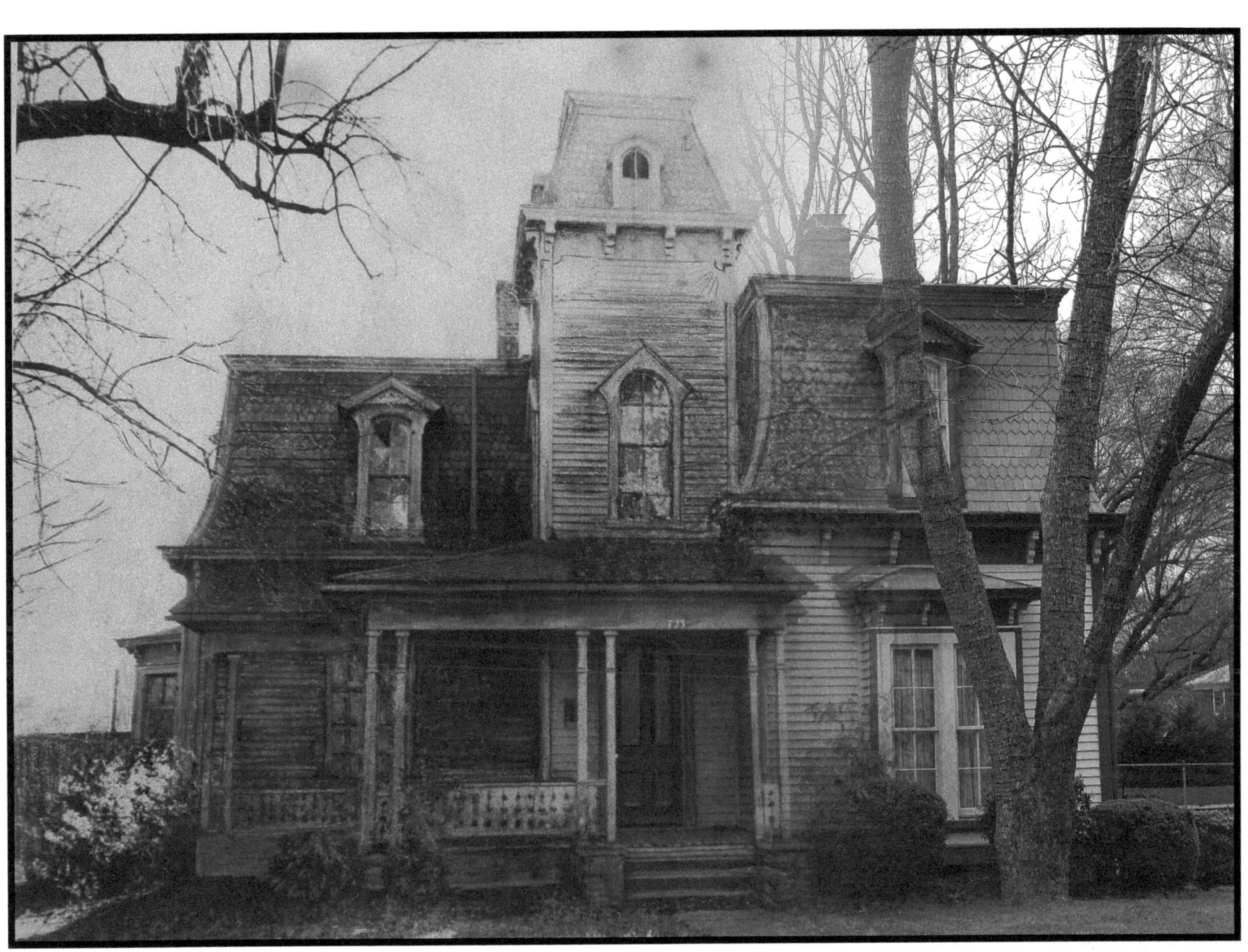

Used To
(Catawba County, NC)

I heard my grandfather once give directions
by telling someone to turn right
where Grady used to keep his goat tied out
beneath that big oak tree on the corner.
By then, though, Grady's goat had been dead
for ten years, Grady, himself, for five,
and the tree had been cut down the year before
to make way for a new gas station.

I still hear people refer to Taste Full Beans
as being across the street from where Cooks used to be.
Of course in the interim, Cooks gave way
to Hometown Sports, and Hometown Sports to Grace Church.
You'd think something that had been there
for 25 years might not have a "Used to,"
but Taste Full Beans used to be Full Circle Arts
and before that a café called The Pleasure Is Mine.

Most old towns are full of "Used Tos":
Moretz, Hollar, and Highland Mills reinvented
as shopping centers or apartments; Bumbargers Books
changed to Bisque 'n Beads; Smith Drugs
to Foot Solutions; Hickory News to Beyond Appearance;
even City Hall changed to the Community Theater;
only here and there you find a Bisanars
selling jewelry in the same place since 1896
still doing things the way they used to.

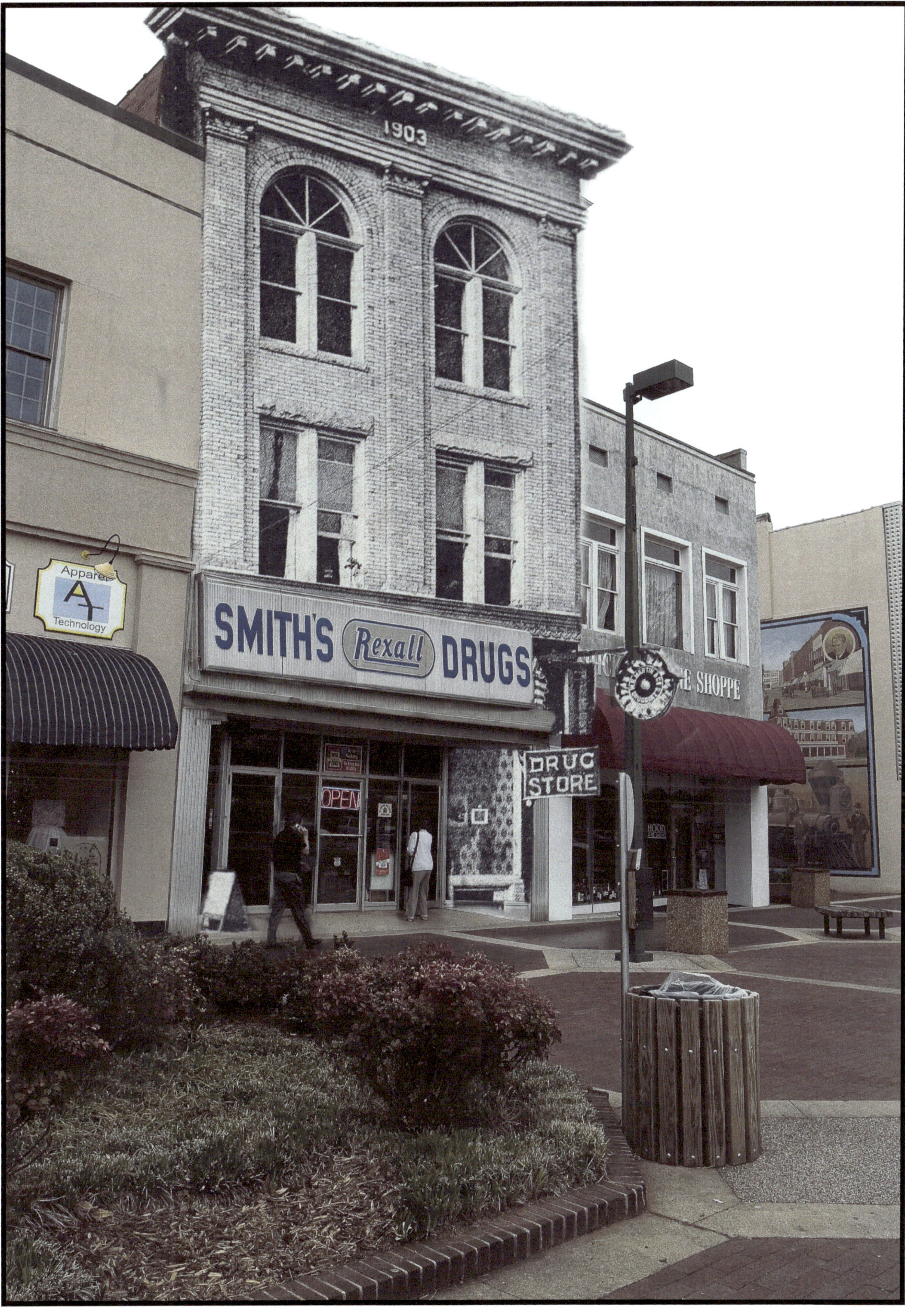
1903
SMITH'S Rexall DRUGS
Apparel
Technology
SHOPPE
DRUG STORE
OPEN

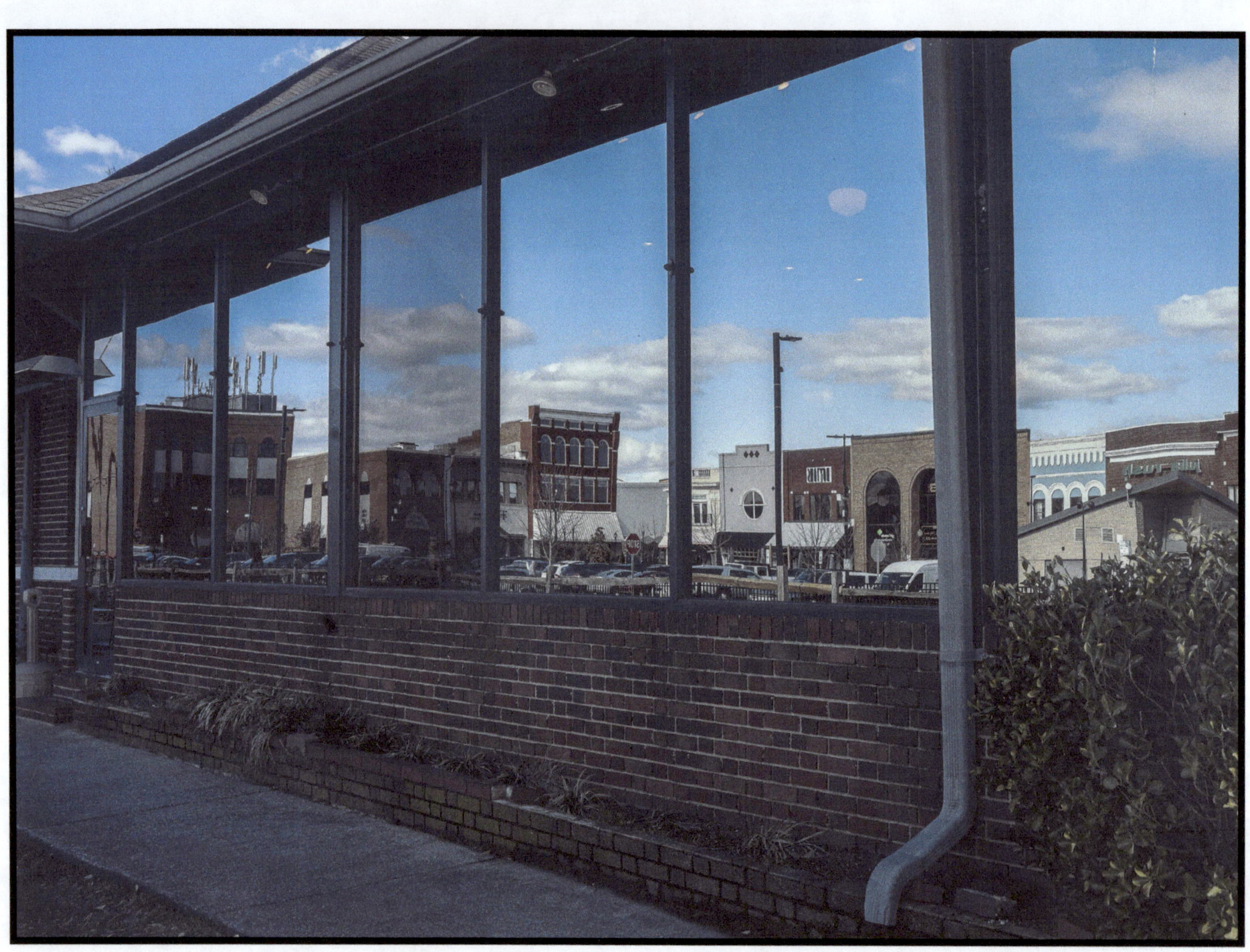

Still

Still
(Catawba County, NC)

RC, JFG, Dr. Pepper, Coca-Cola,
Owl Cigars, Woolworth's, Mr. Peanut, Faygo Orange,
Mail Pouch, Bull Durham, John Deere,
Brecht Candies, Wrigley's Doublemint, Dad's Root Beer,
not manufactured on plastic or laminate
in some distant plant but painted
on brick on the side of a shop, salon, bus terminal,
as if intended to stay there more than a year or two,
subtle denial of impermanence.

I've got no problem with the artsy murals
going up everywhere today, but sometimes
I long for the simplicity of straightforward
advertising, no emotional manipulation
of cute children or cuter pets,
no digital projections or rotating screens,
not even lights to demand our attention,
simply name recognition, standing still,
a simpler sign of simpler times.

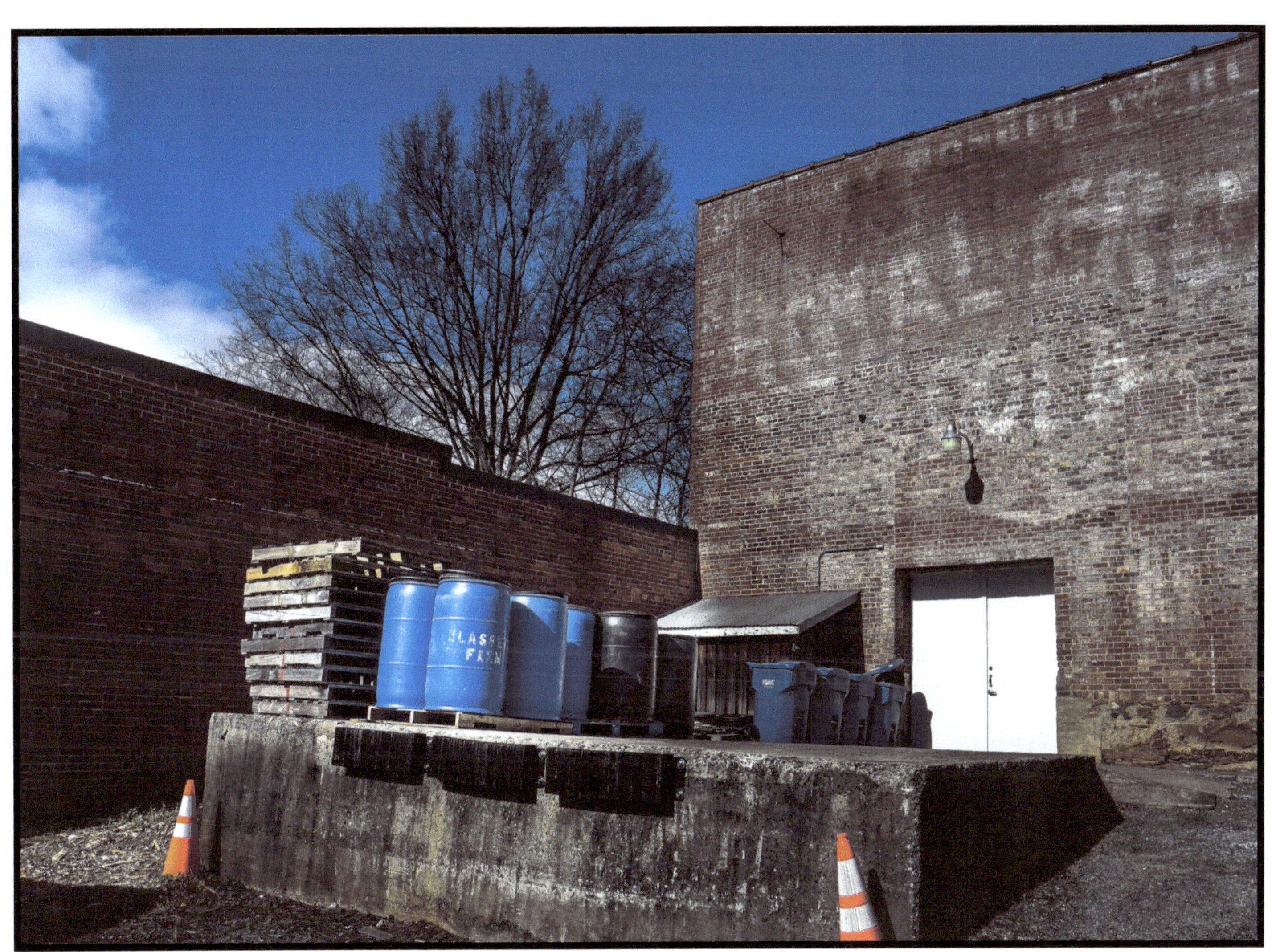

Walking the Tracks
(Catawba County, NC)

Walking the tracks from east or west
you see the backs of people's yards,
you see life not as they're told
it should be, prepared, planned, orchestrated,
but as it really is, clothes lines
and big wheels, plastic swimming pools,
and then, getting closer, the buildings appear,
the old ones, the ones that needed to be next
to the tracks, the Granary, Piedmont Wagon,
Lyerly Mill, Old Hickory Station,
where Theodore Roosevelt stumped in 1912,
the grounds before, even the tops
of railcars packed with those who came
to see the great man who came to Hickory.
As far as anyone living could tell
the tracks have always been there
and probably always will.

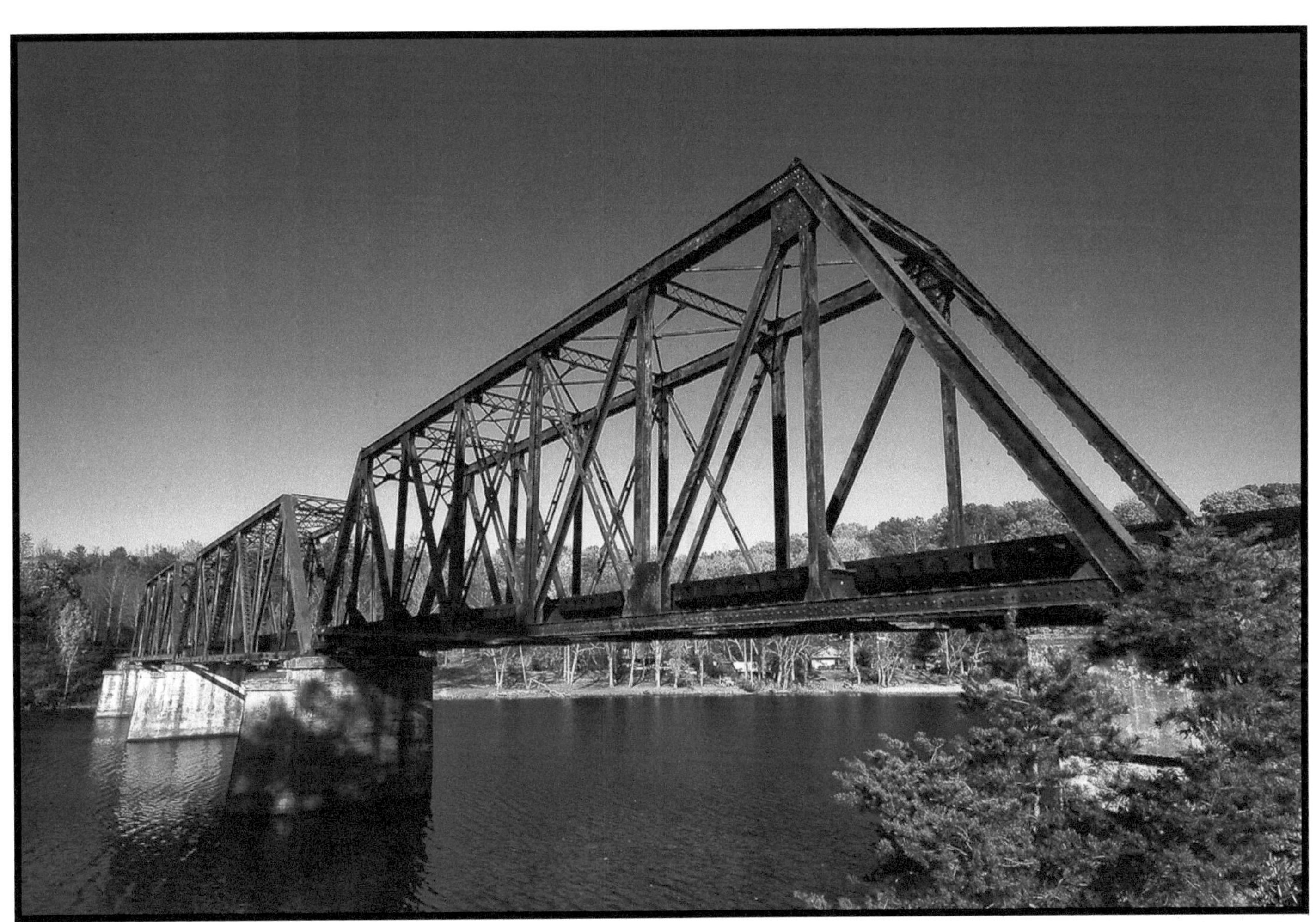

Shopkeeper
(Catawba County, NC)

Sweeping the walkway in front of the shop
he remembers 50 years ago
sweeping the walkway in front of White's Grocery.
Barely 8 and having no money
but wanting chocolate, he asked
if there was anything he could do
for a Snickers Bar. And being told *"No,"*
he came back the next day
and asked again and kept asking
every day until Mr. White
said, *"Okay. You do it and then*
come back to me and if you do
a good job you will have chocolate
and you will come back tomorrow
and do a good job and have chocolate
and keep coming back until you learn
what has to be learned, until learning
becomes habit."

Now the same back and forth motion
of arms takes him back to making things
clean, to finding his way, to learning
what had to be learned,
to earning what has to be earned.

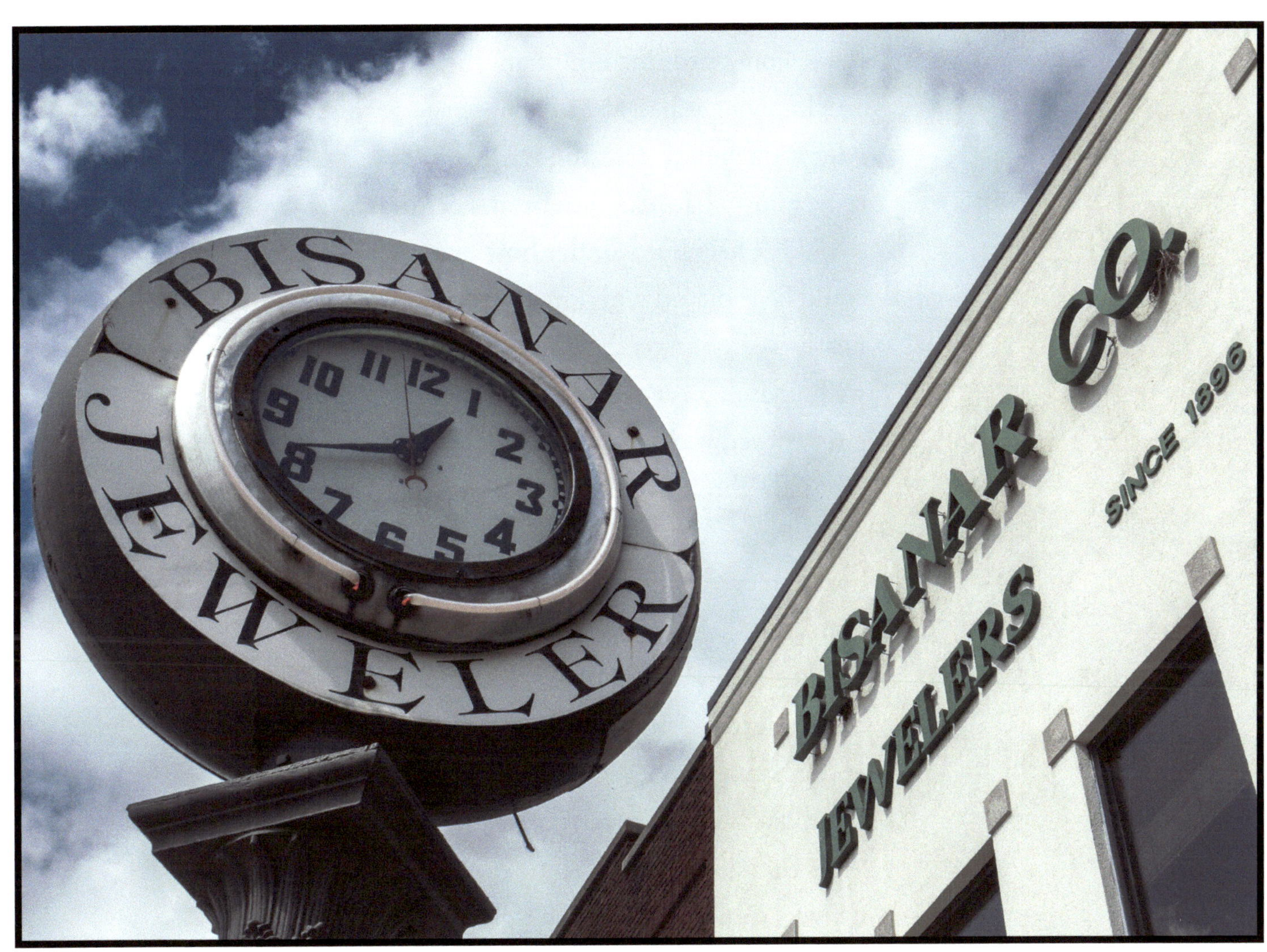
BISANAR
JEWELERS
BISANAR CO.
JEWELERS
SINCE 1896

Reclamation

(Catawba County, NC)

Having seen the transformation of one
rundown textile mill into expensive
restaurant, brewery, boutique shops
for clothes and frozen yogurt, and noticing
the ongoing cleaning out of another,
and knowing it had already happened with my life,
education and divorce and writing
redeeming what had once been worthless,
I couldn't help but wonder how much
could be achieved with any body
nearly worn out, teeth straightened
with invisalign, eyes fixed by laser,
gut restored with probiotics,
foot pain eliminated by the Strassburg Sock,

but then even after rejuvenation,
even among the young, it's not always
pretty, not always full of grace,
the crude, oil-stained nuts and bolts
of life, the unphotogenic face,
a bad day that keeps getting worse,
walls that don't line up, some bricks
uneven, some not quite the right size,
and that's what the mortar's for,
the gray areas of tolerance,
forgiveness, understanding,
empathetic appreciation of things
being left imperfect, only as good
as we can stand to make them be.

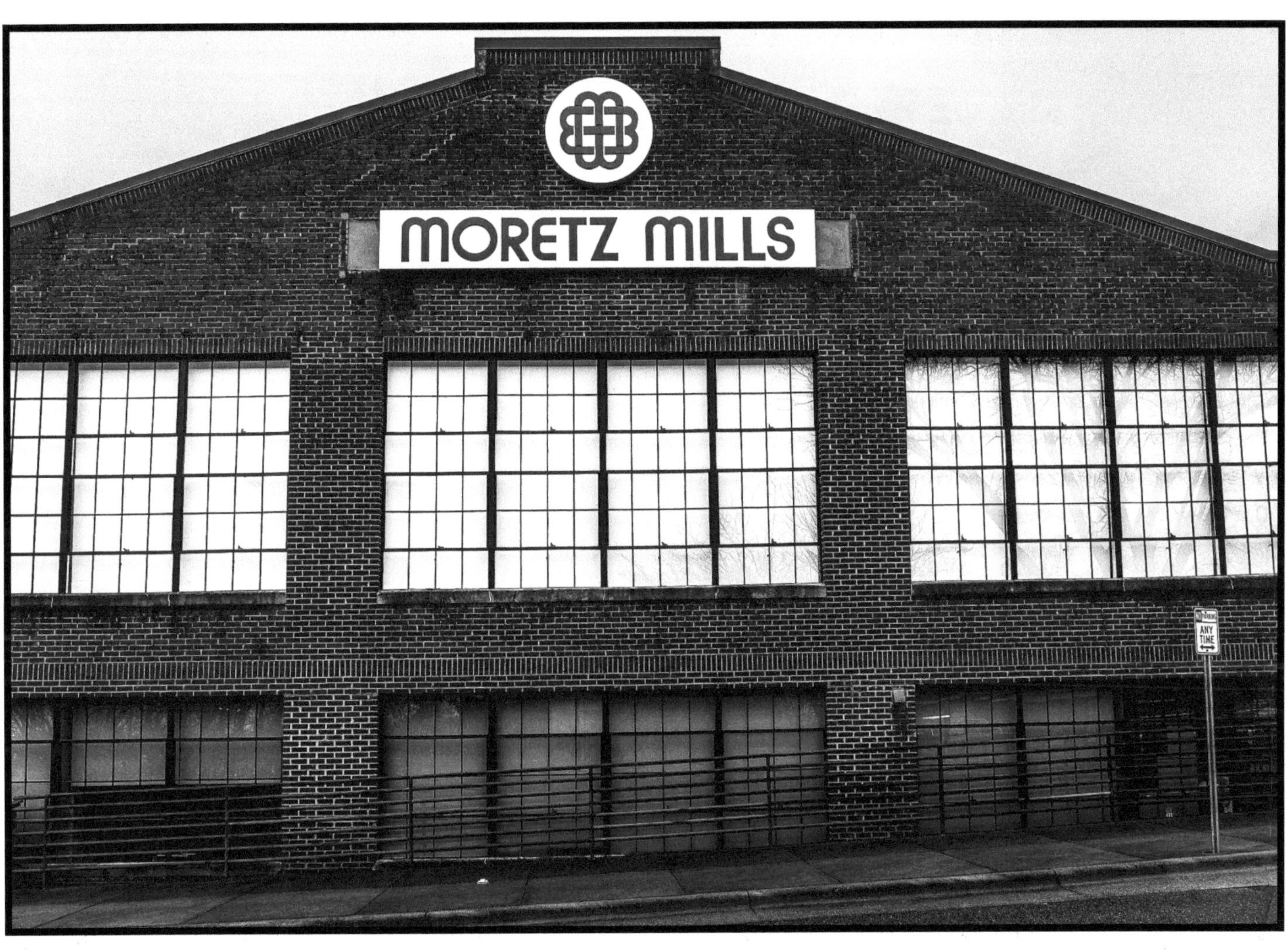
MORETZ MILLS
ANY TIME

A Study of Steeples
(Catawba County, NC)

What Southern church worth its name would be
without one?
Spire, tower, obelisk, pillar, pole,
bellhouse, minaret, place to hang a light from,
meant to inspire, conspire, transpire, aspire,
virile symbol of strength, suggested rising
towards better things, ever-pointing towards where
we most imagine God to be, heaven
to be, protection against what might descend,
architectural banner rising above treetops,
housetops, city walls -- what first drew us
to this house of possibility and drew our eyes
upwards to what always seemed a stormy sky
and made us think that maybe this could be
an inverted funnel to take us almost anywhere else.

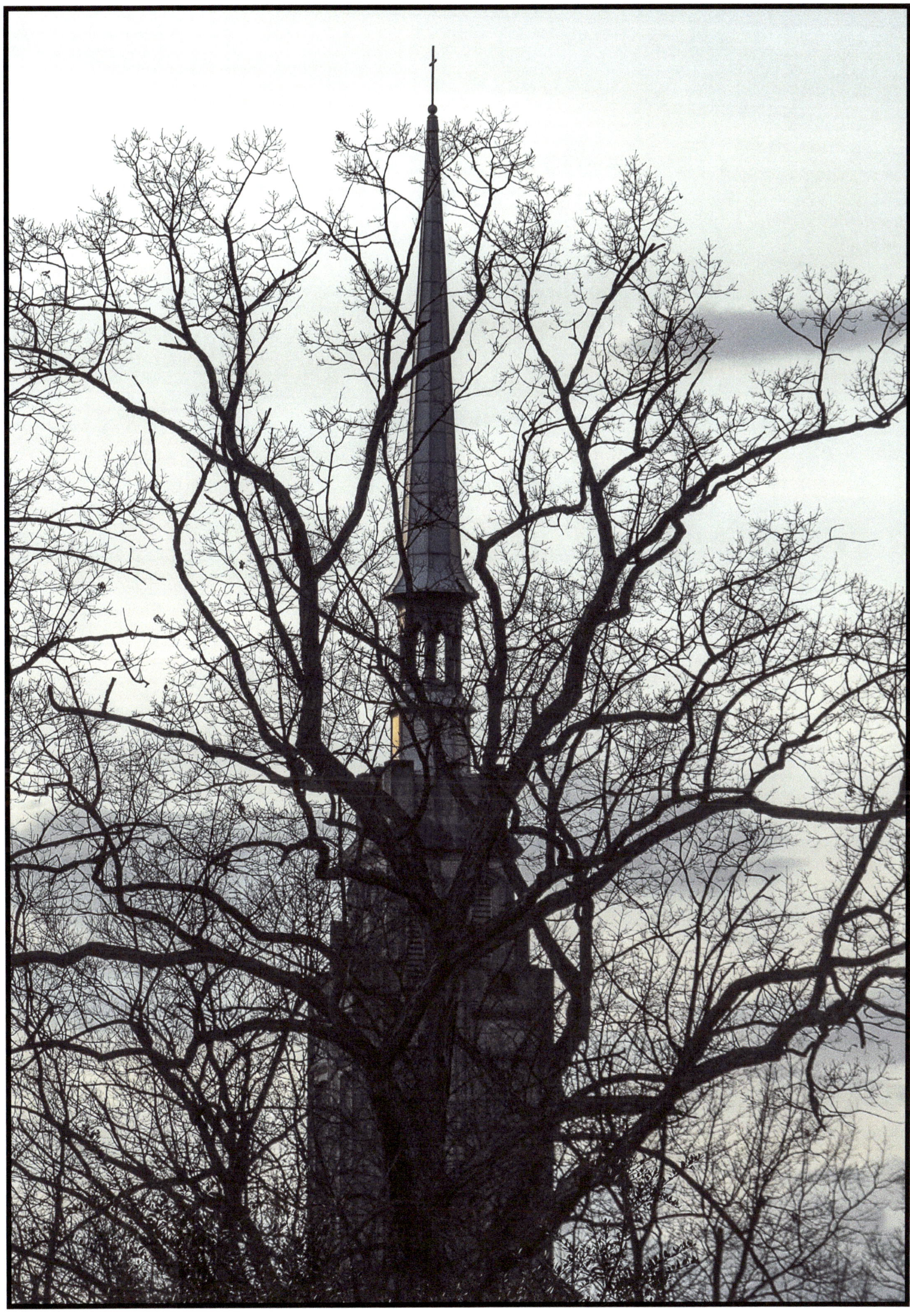

Pinwheel
(Catawba County, NC)

What little girl wouldn't want
something to twirl, whirligig,
spinning top, hula hoop?
My own daughter wouldn't wear
a dress unless she could spin it.
Here, in this place of play for all children,
2001 pinwheels, mostly paper,
spinning in wind make
a persistent flutter like children
laughing, running, playing.
And this one, metal, stronger,
bigger, permanent, but still spinning,
memorial to a childhood cut short
even before it ended,
to all childhoods interrupted
by violence, left to remind us
the childhood joy seen
in motion, color, play,
breathless wonder.

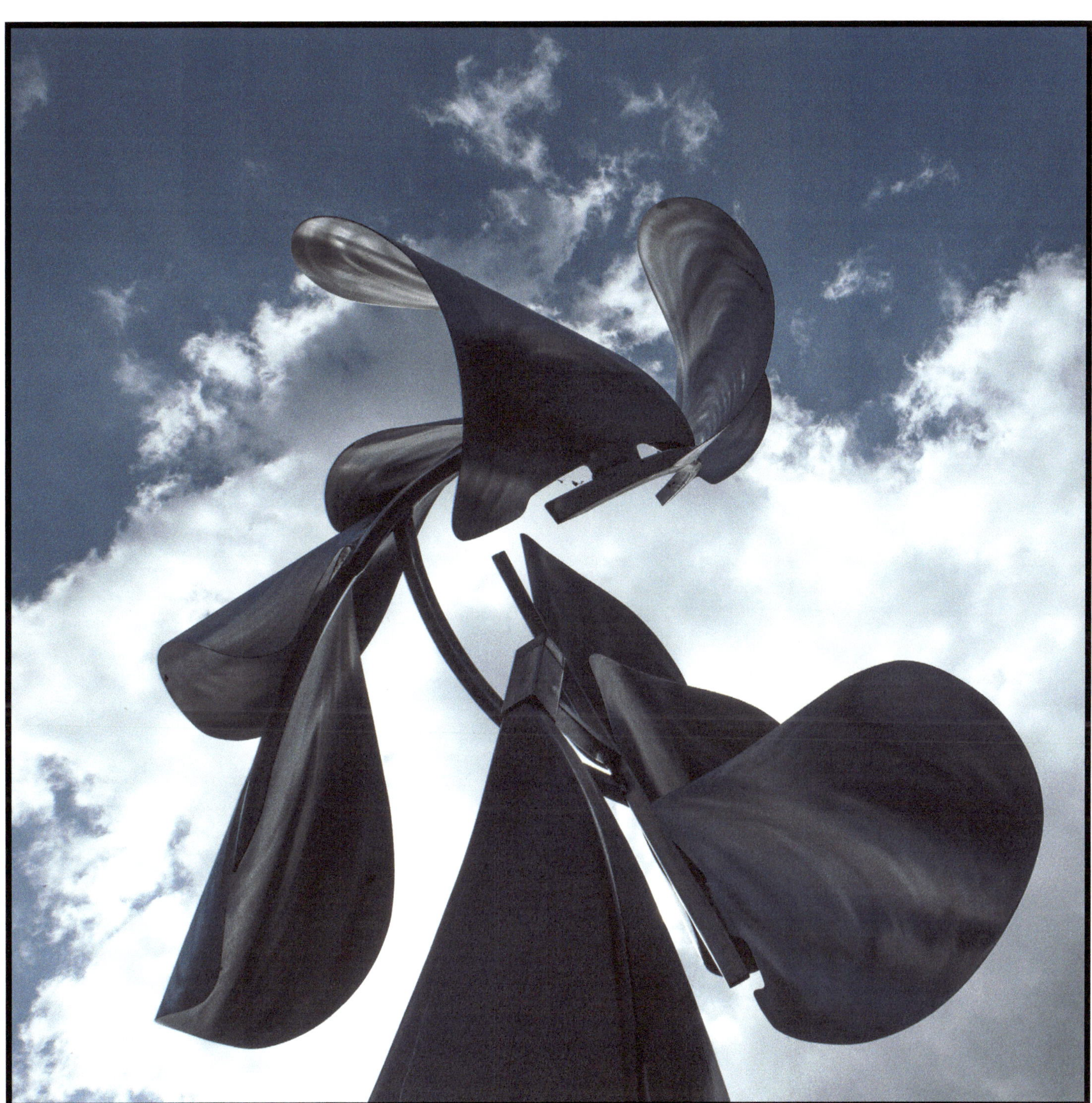

memorial day –
reading names of those who roared
as loud as cannons

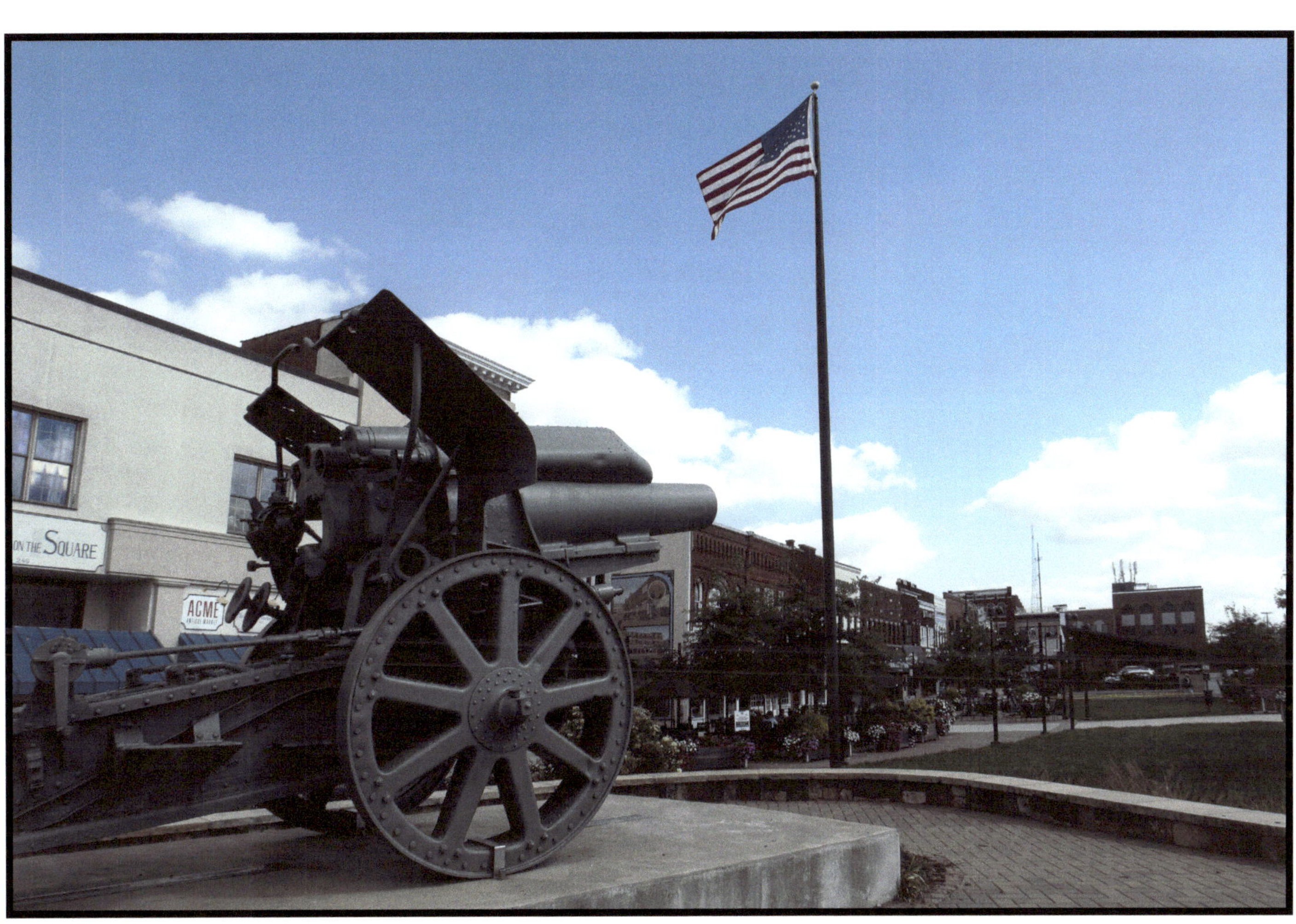
ON THE SQUARE
ACME

Coffee During Covid

(Catawba County, NC)

It's not the same, of course.
Students don't unpack at the table,
linger for hours, doing homework,
sipping on a single almond milk latte;
friends don't gather around,
sharing stories, getting refills,
trying Guatemalan, Costa Rican,
West Java Siliwangi.
The shop doesn't bustle
with the hustle of a steady flow,
drip or press, constant espress.
More a slow come and go
of customers you already know
and knew would show no matter
the long distress of lasting woe.

Still, when you feel the chill
of autumn's coming on,
in a time of greater solitude,
lesser solace, uncertain hope,
a cup of coffee in the quiet cold
of morning can be a breath
of calm reassurance,
can feel something
like sudden comfort,
Dark Bliss, Cup of Joy,
Glorious Morning.

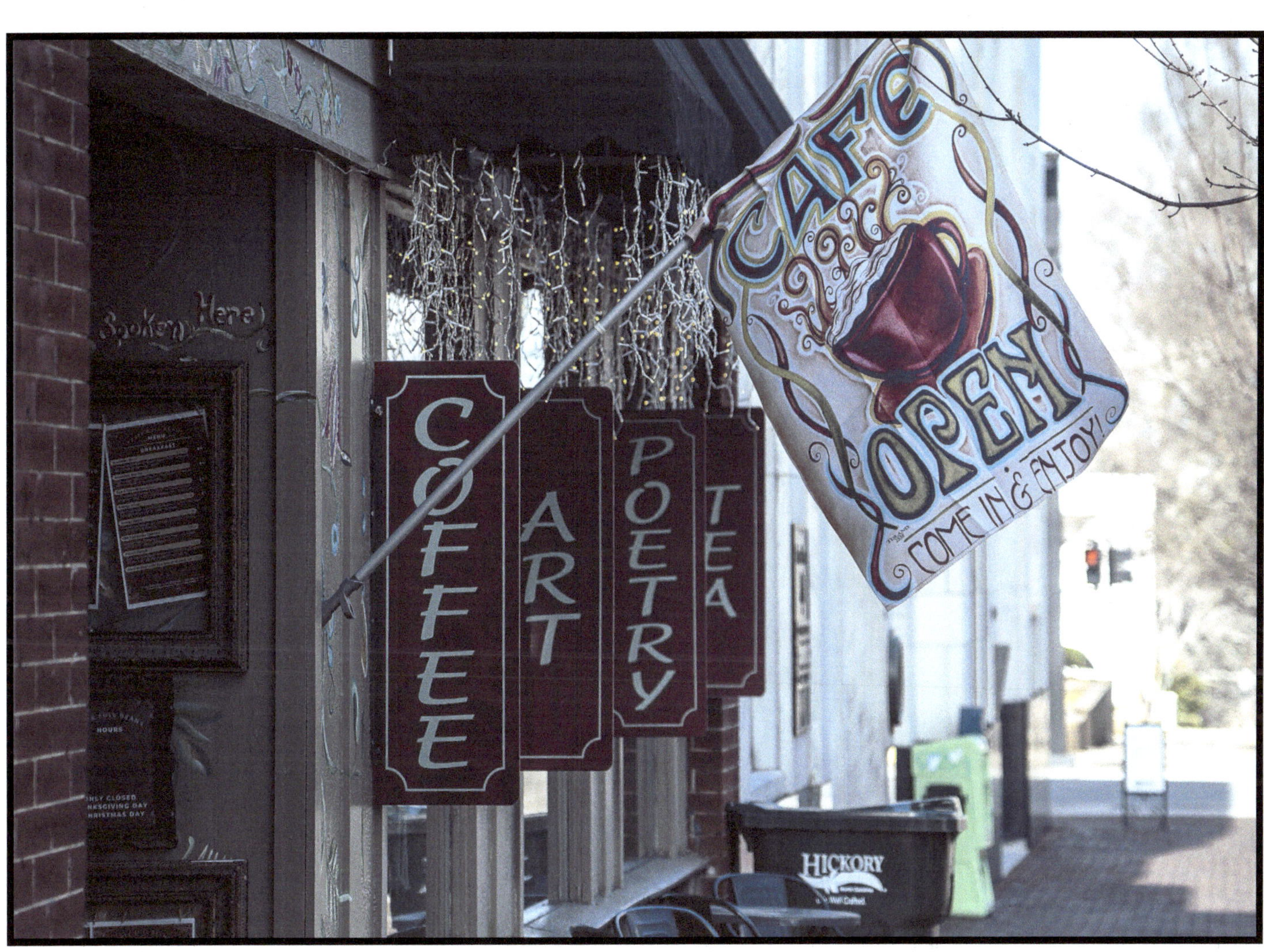
Spoken Here
COFFEE
ART
POETRY
TEA
CAFE
OPEN
COME IN & ENJOY!
HICKORY

Secrets of Southern Sweet Tea

(Mecklenburg County, NC)

Everyone who came to eat at my grandmother's house
had to answer the same question before they were served,
Jaunt drank or jaunt tay,
drank being whatever soda was in the fridge at the time,
usually whatever had been on sale at the Bi Lo that week,
and *tay* being tea, but not just any old tea,
my grandmother's sweet, Southern iced tea,
and anyone who knew anything about my grandmother
would loosen their belts and answer *Tay*.
Twice as strong as the box called for,
a pinch of baking soda added while steeping,
at least a cup of sugar per gallon,
tea bags finally removed, and let drip
in the pot but not squeezed,
then the whole thing poured into gallon mason jars
and chilled in the fridge for at least four hours
but preferably over night. Served in tall, thick-sided glasses
with lots of ice (made this strong, extra ice could never hurt it).
I would add that you should never keep it for more than a week
but when it tasted as good as hers that was never a concern.

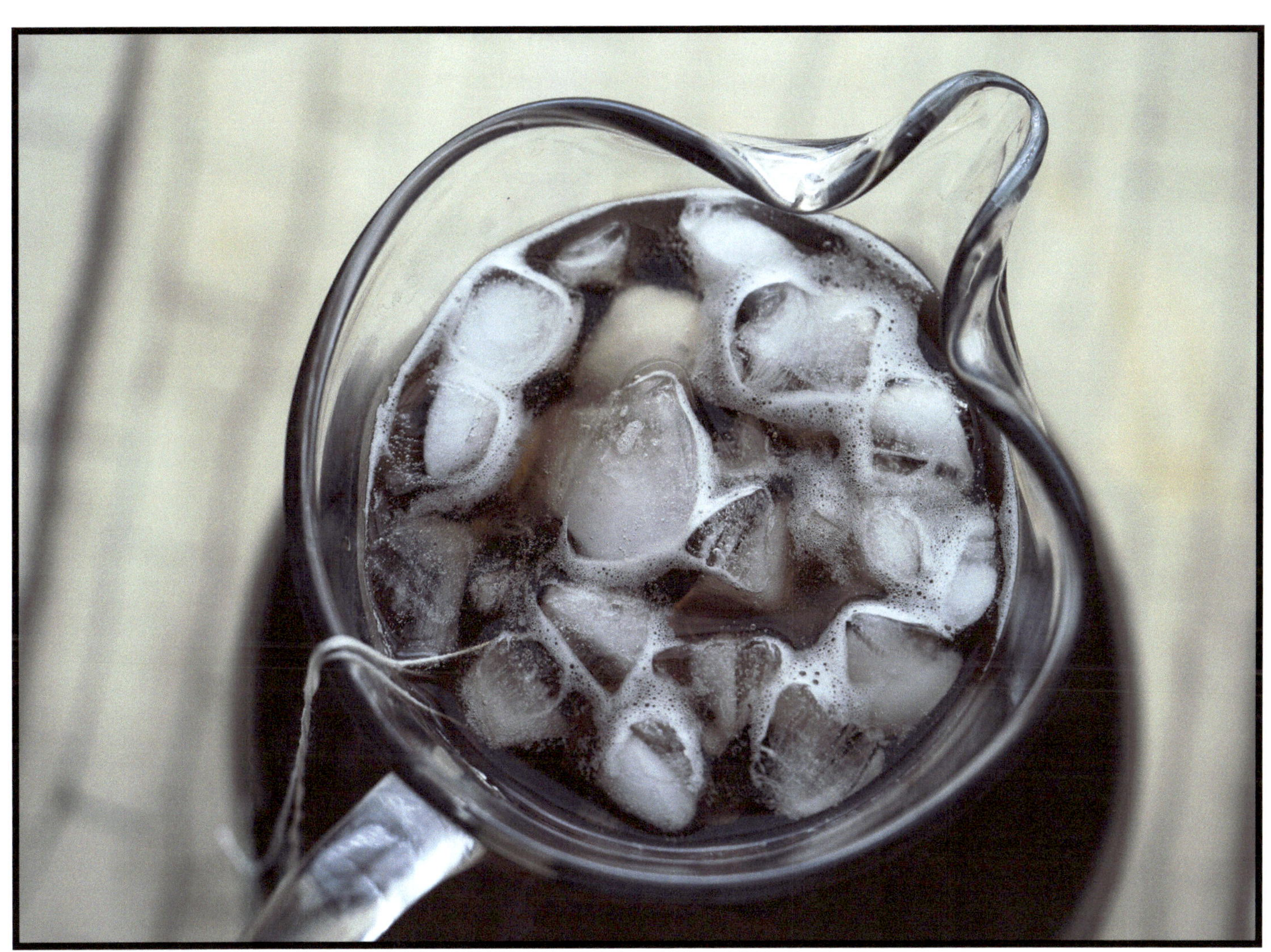

Address

(Catawba County, NC)

I live at 838 4th Avenue Drive Northwest.
I love the specificity of the place,
the 38th lot in the 8th block
of not a street but an avenue,
an avenue that alone is not enough
to hold me, but rather an avenue
in the crosshairs of avenue and drive,
and not just any avenue either,
but specifically the fourth avenue
in the northwest quadrant of a town
in North Carolina, on the continent
of North America, in the Northern Hemisphere
of the third planet from the sun
in the Orion Arm of the Milky Way,
somewhere in the little we know
of the known Universe, and I need
all of this to know where I am,
and to know the importance of the particular,
and to know that no matter how broad my thinking,
no matter how far-reaching my knowledge
or ideas, I can always only live
in one particular place
at one particular time.

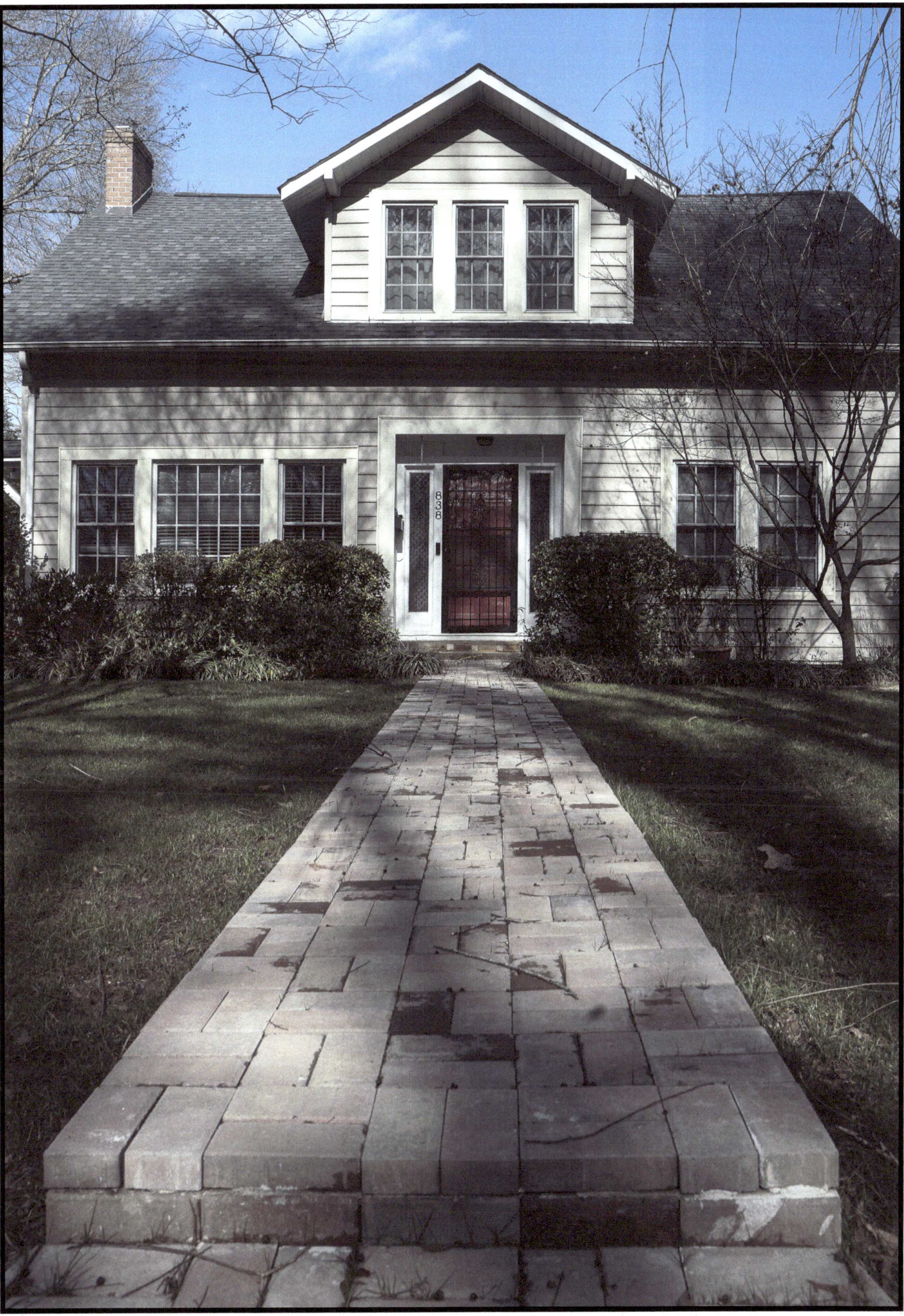
838

Thinking about the Next Big Bang in the Galaxy at the Edge of Town

(Catawba County, NC)

In the Galaxy at the edge of town
there is still plenty of fresh air,
space is abundant, light
is spread evenly everywhere.

Children keep rattling wheels
moving forward, the machinery
of produce continues,
seven languages are spoken.

A homeless man seeks shelter,
jacket pulled tight around him,
orbs of eyes concealed
beneath rings of his hat's brim.

Stockboys wait for beauty
to descend and need them, they dream
constellations in their hands,
spin cans to face the front.

Potentialities, polarities, cosmic
design are all worked out
in the commerce of heavenly bodies.
Everything moves in perpetual orbit.

A man walking between rows
wonders at the infinity of choice
spread out before him, thinks
one day decisions won't matter.

At closing time they walk
towards the black hole
of windows, afraid of no
gravity but their own.

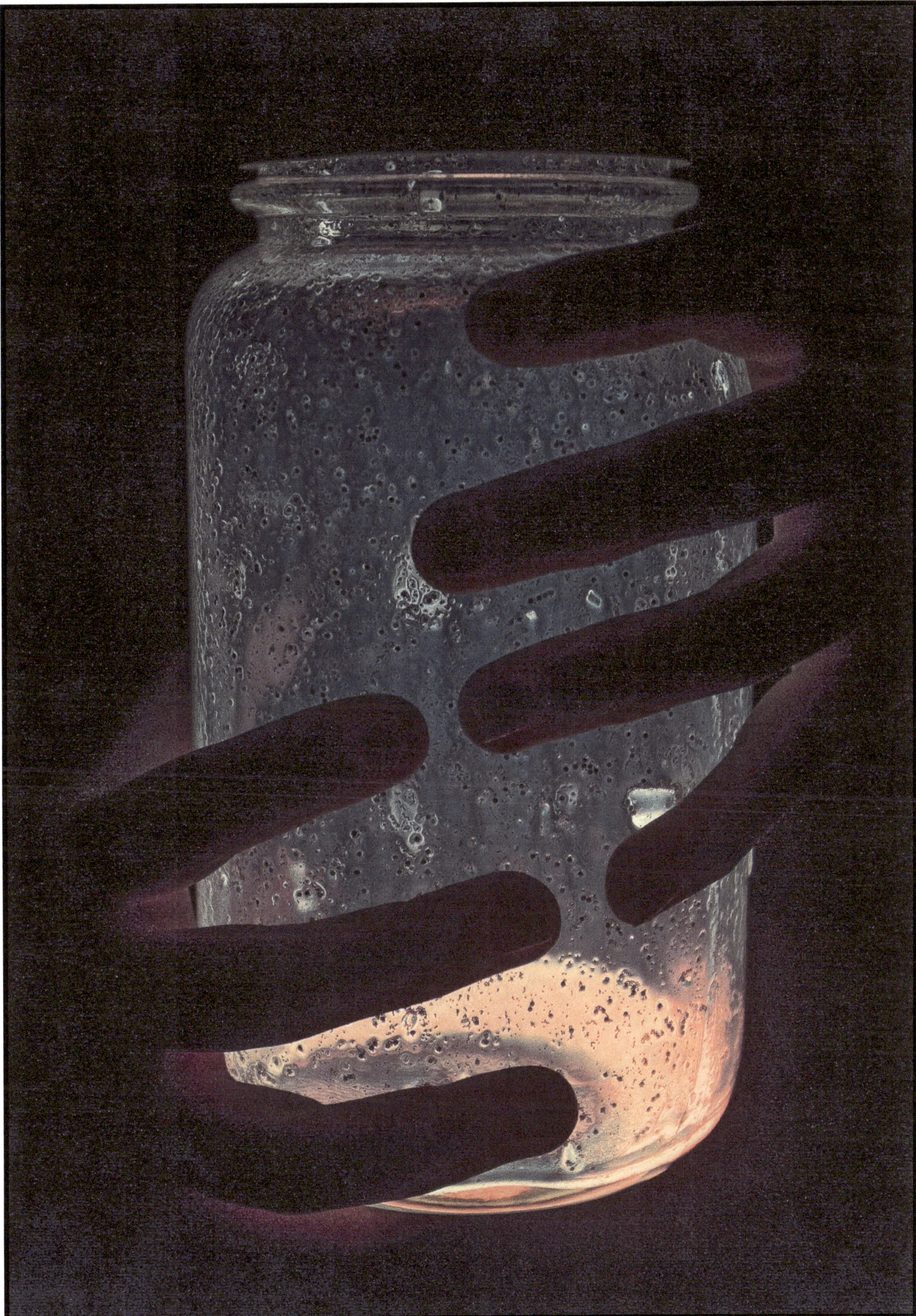

Why So Many of Those Who Are Lost in Hickory Stay That Way Forever

(Catawba County, NC)

Those who are lost in Hickory
can count on the streets of Hickory
to lose them further forever.
I, for example, live
near the intersection
of 4th Avenue Drive NW
(which becomes 10th Street Place NW,
which doesn't connect with the other
five streets named 10th Street Place NW)
and 4th Avenue NW (which doesn't connect
with 4th Avenue NE but does intersect
with 4th Street NW which becomes
4th Street Drive NW without requiring a turn).

No one who lives here refers to the streets
by name. If you want to find the coffee shop
where we hold poetry readings, for example,
they'll tell you it's across from where Cook's
used to be which became Hometown Sports
before it moved to Main Avenue NE
and 6th Street Place SE where it isn't anymore.

And if you want to go to the Shurtape plant,
and you're on Main Ave. NE, which becomes
8th St. NE, which is also LR Blvd,
you can turn at King Hickory,
where it intersects with Highland Ave.,
which is also 8th St. NE, being careful
to choose the second of four roads
from the right at the next intersection
so you don't wind up on 8th Ave. NE
which would take you back to 8th St. NE

or to Main Ave. NE which doesn't connect
to the Main Ave. NE you started out on.
What mad engineer one might wonder
drunk on power or a sick sense of humor
thought any town needed
an intersection of Second and Second
and two straight blocks later
the same named intersection again?
Or felt it necessary that to stay on 2nd Street SE,
driving north from Highway 70
should require one to turn right on Highway 127,
then magically leap two blocks east
back onto 2nd Street SE,
then turn right on 5th Avenue SE
and left on 2nd Street Place SE
and left again on 3rd Avenue SE
and right again back onto 2nd Street SE,
then right on 2nd Avenue SE,
and left once again onto 2nd Street SE,
then left on 1st Avenue SE
and right once more onto 2nd Street SE
being careful not to turn too soon
onto 2nd Street Place SE,
all of which will eventually intersect 2nd Avenue NE
after merging with 2nd Street Drive NE
and then become North Center Street
which it runs parallel to
before North Center Street deadends
temporarily into 2nd Street Place NE,
taking up the name North Center Street
again after a right and a left
but finally leaving any indication
of Second behind it as it becomes
simply Highway 127 once again
and heads decidedly out of town
and back into some semblance of sanity.

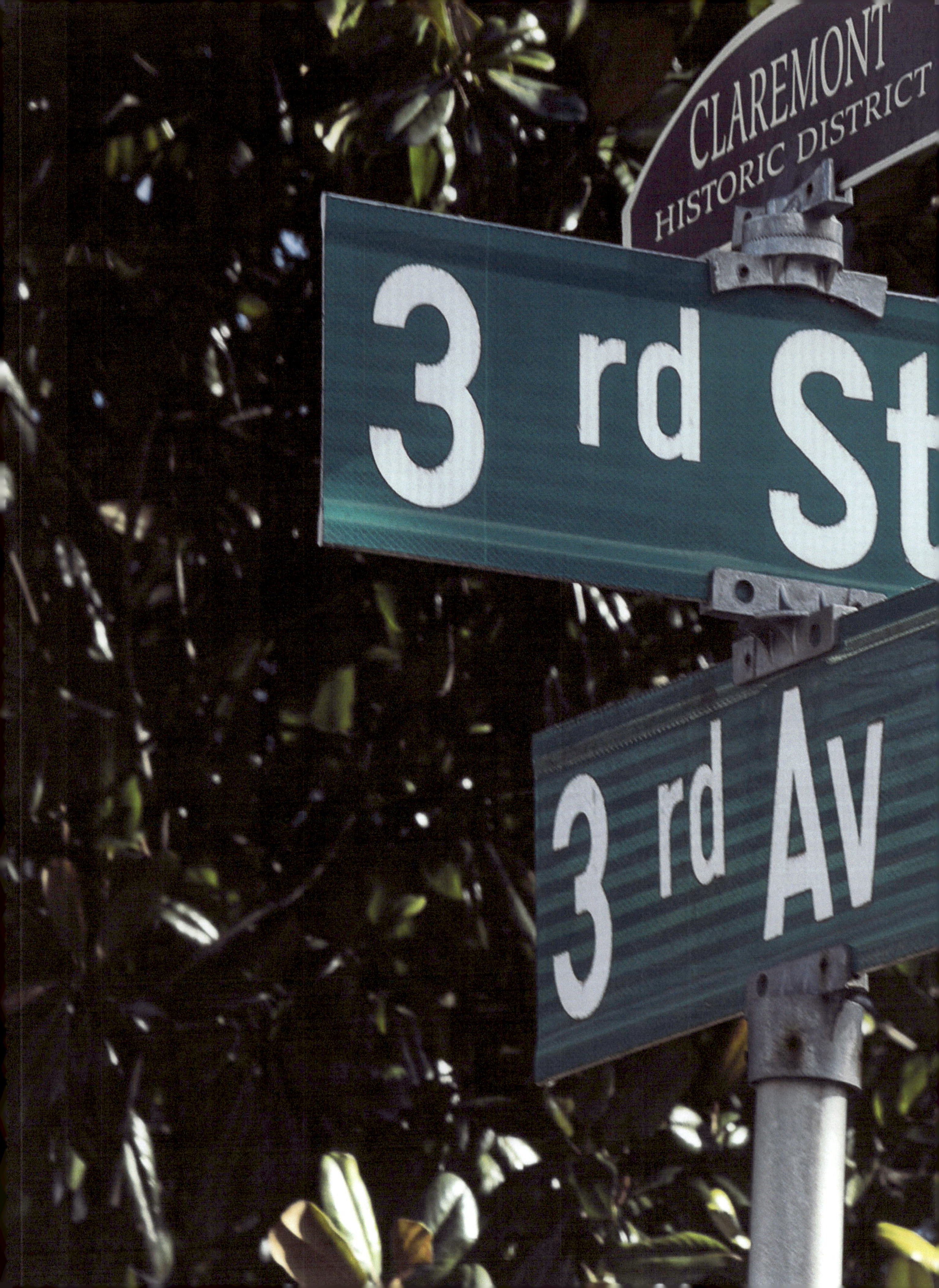

CLAREMONT
HISTORIC DISTRICT
3 rd St
3 rd Av

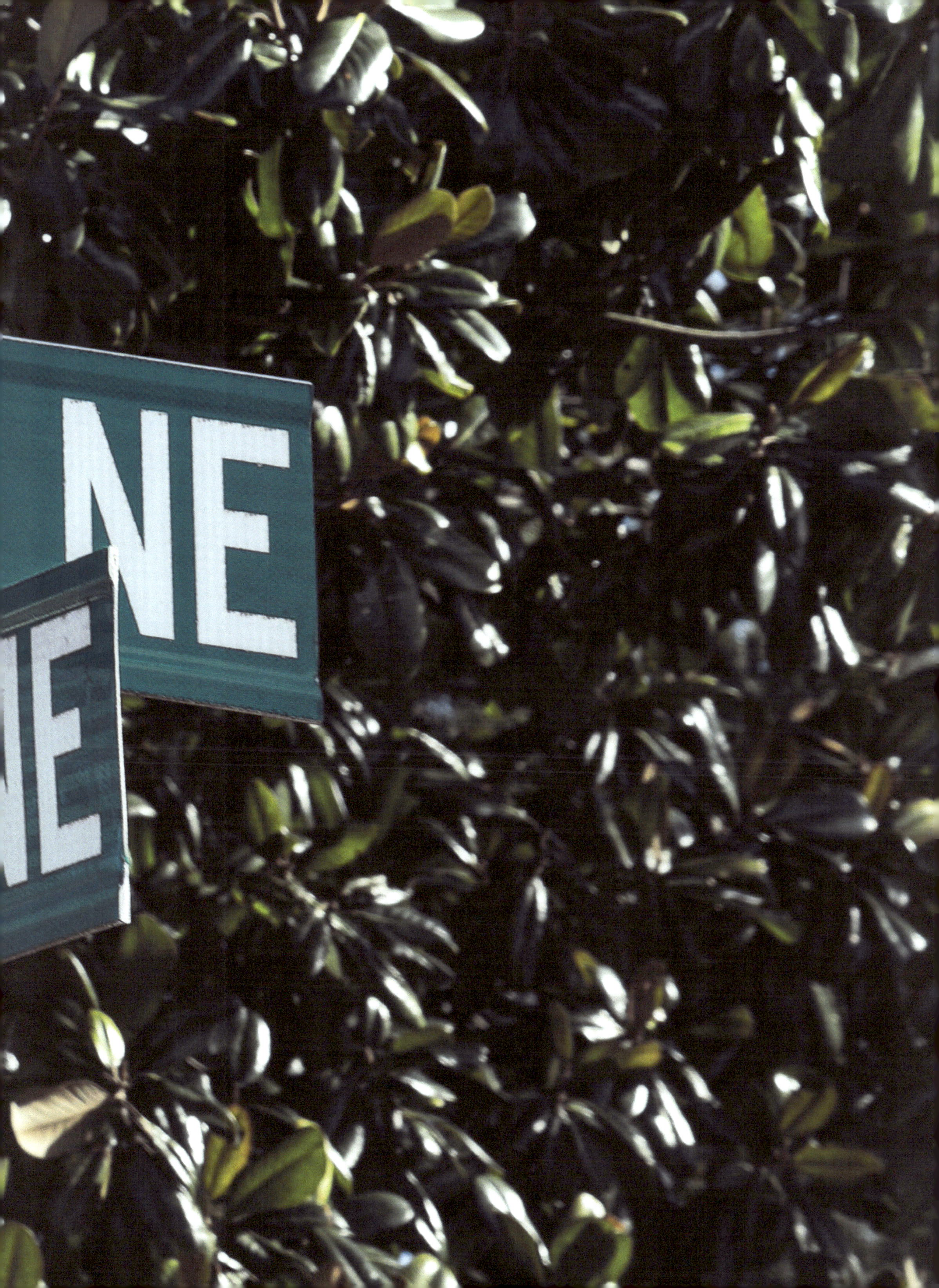
NE

Chapel
(Catawba County, NC)

Fifty-four windows point up,
Most of them stained glass , every roof line,
decorative support, every doorway,
and inside, the same windows,
and 8 peaked arches rising 60 feet
from cool stone to a forest of timber above.
How could anyone resist such a muscular
religion so full of the promise of ascension
embodied in a place where only light descends?

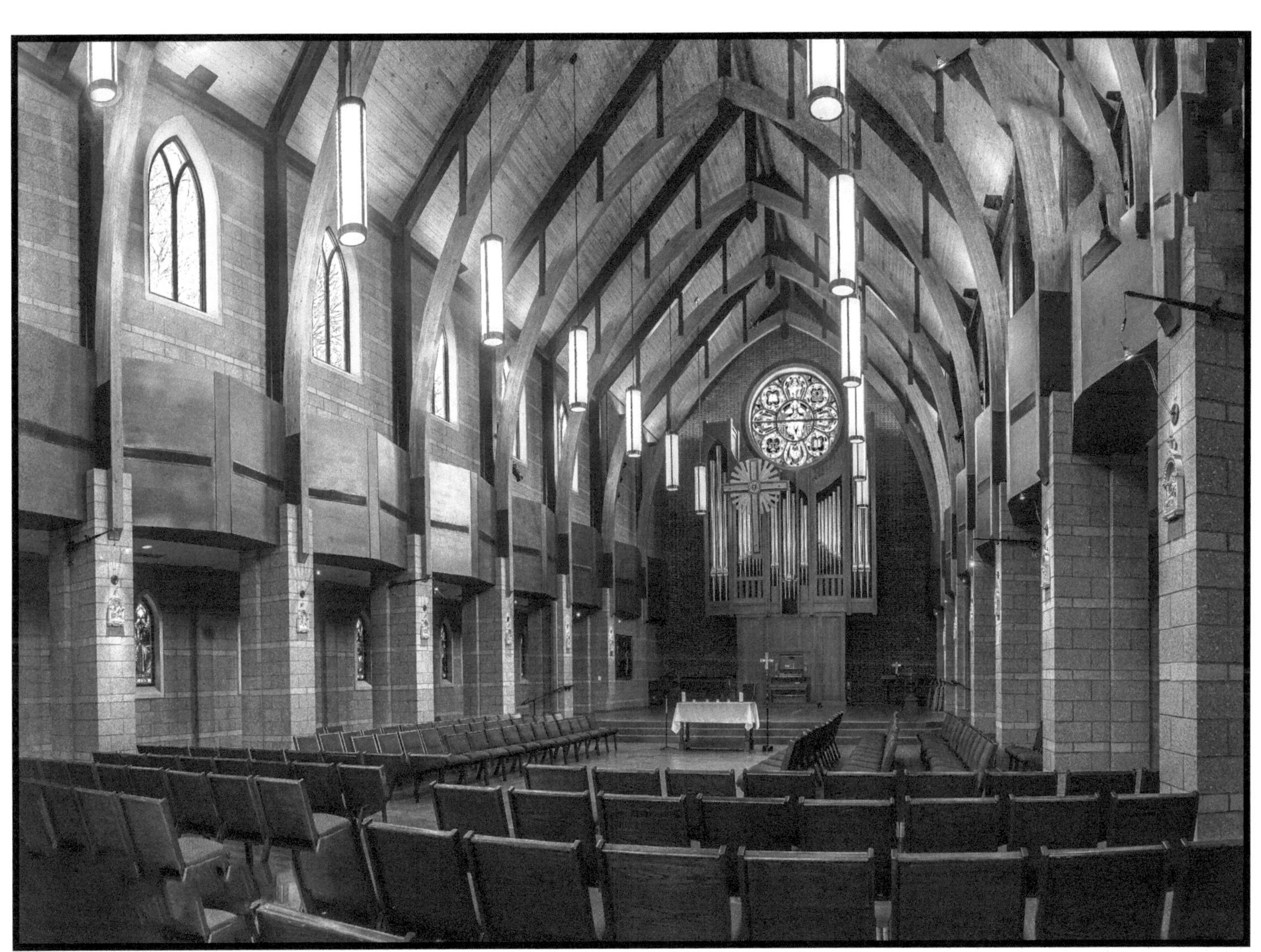

Art Appreciation
(Catawba County, NC)

I take twenty-three students,
ages six to eleven,
to the Hickory Museum of Art
and tell them about ekphrastic
poetry and how the word
ekphrasis comes from Greek
and has to do with calling out
the true name and hence
the true meaning of a work
of art and teach them how
to write a poem about
a work of art by noticing
color and shape and form
and other more beautiful things
like memory, meaning, association.
The museum is full of beautiful
works of art with beautiful
names like *Blue Skies,*
Spring Thaw, Color-Blind Angel,
and it is sheer joy watching
twenty-three young people
marvel at art and reflect
on the possibilities of creation,
but my daughter, because she is eight
and curious about all things,
because she is eight and believes
boundaries exist to be pushed,
because she is eight
and wouldn't waste a chance
to say a bad word and not
get into trouble, looks
long and hard at every
beautiful work of art,
at every beautiful name
before choosing to write
about James Harold Jennings'
Bad Girl Beats Hell Out of the Devil.

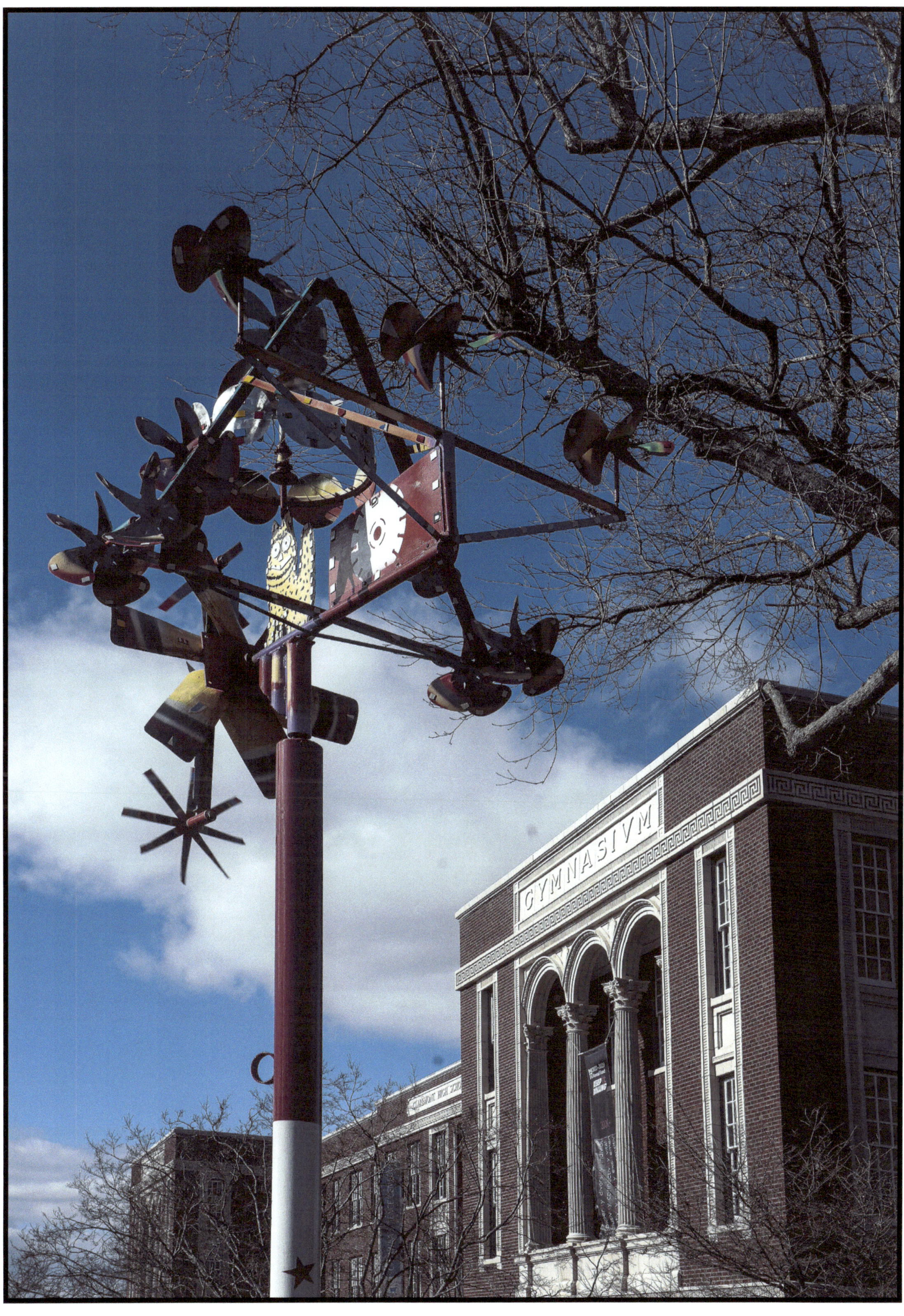
GYMNASIVM
CLAREMONT HIGH SCHO

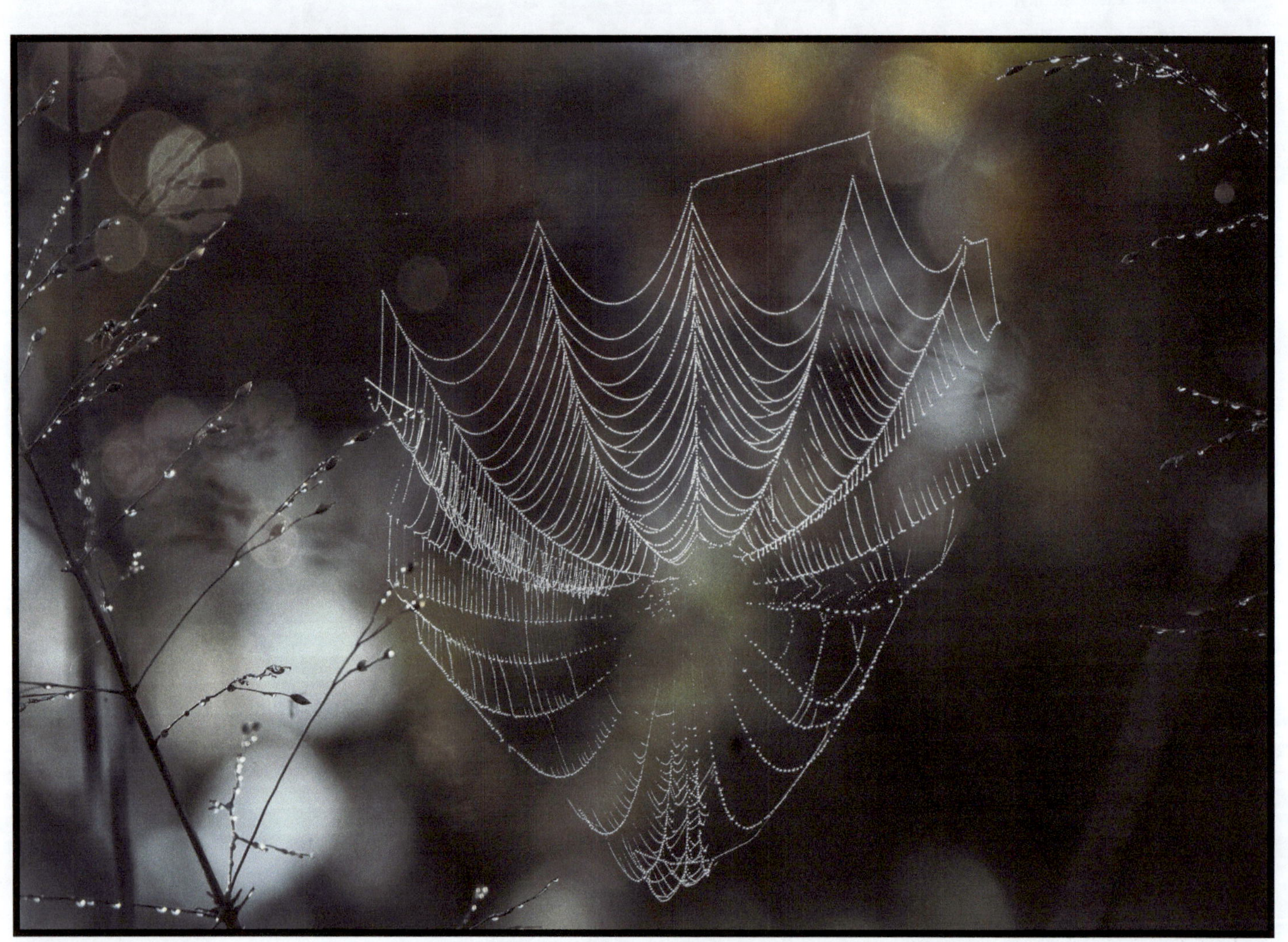

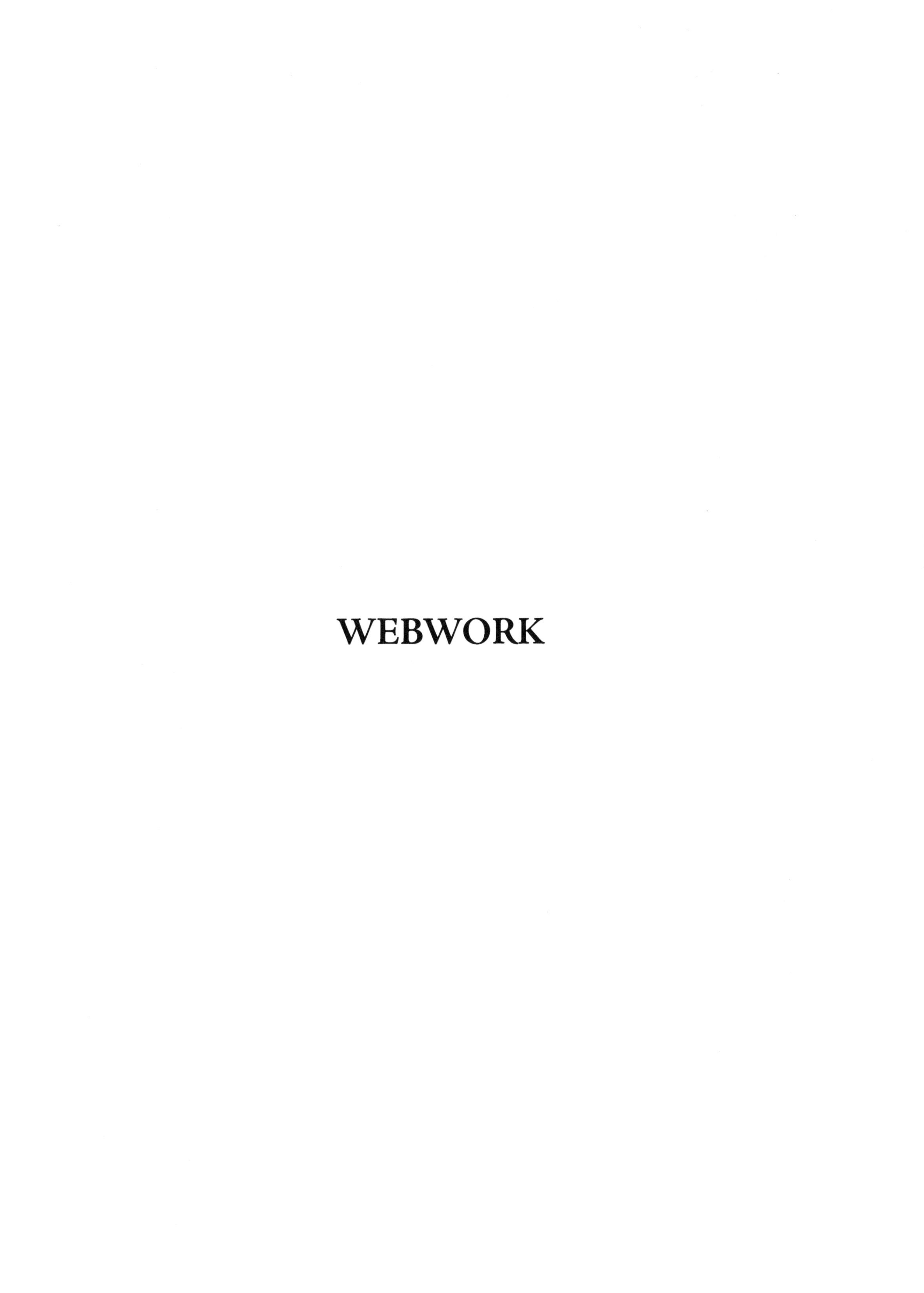

WEBWORK

The Urbanization of Trails

(Catawba County, NC)

It all started as trails,
trade routes north to south
and east to west, connecting
Saponi and Cherokee,
Waxhaw and Catawba.
So maybe it's only natural
that everyone walks around here.
For years we walked our neighborhoods,
Oakwood, and Hillcrest,
Kentwood, and Lakeland Park,
or walked the trails of Glenn Hilton,
Bakers Mountain, Riverbend,
Geitner, Henry Fork.
Now, in the Year of the Trail,
the trails have come closer again,
and we walk wide thoroughfares,
pedestrian bridges, lined with benches,
beneath trees and good lighting.
City Walk,
Art Walk,
Book Walk,
Aviation Walk,
River Walk,
ten miles in all,
all doing what trails were always meant to do,
getting people up and outside,
in the air, beneath the sun,
joining one place to another.

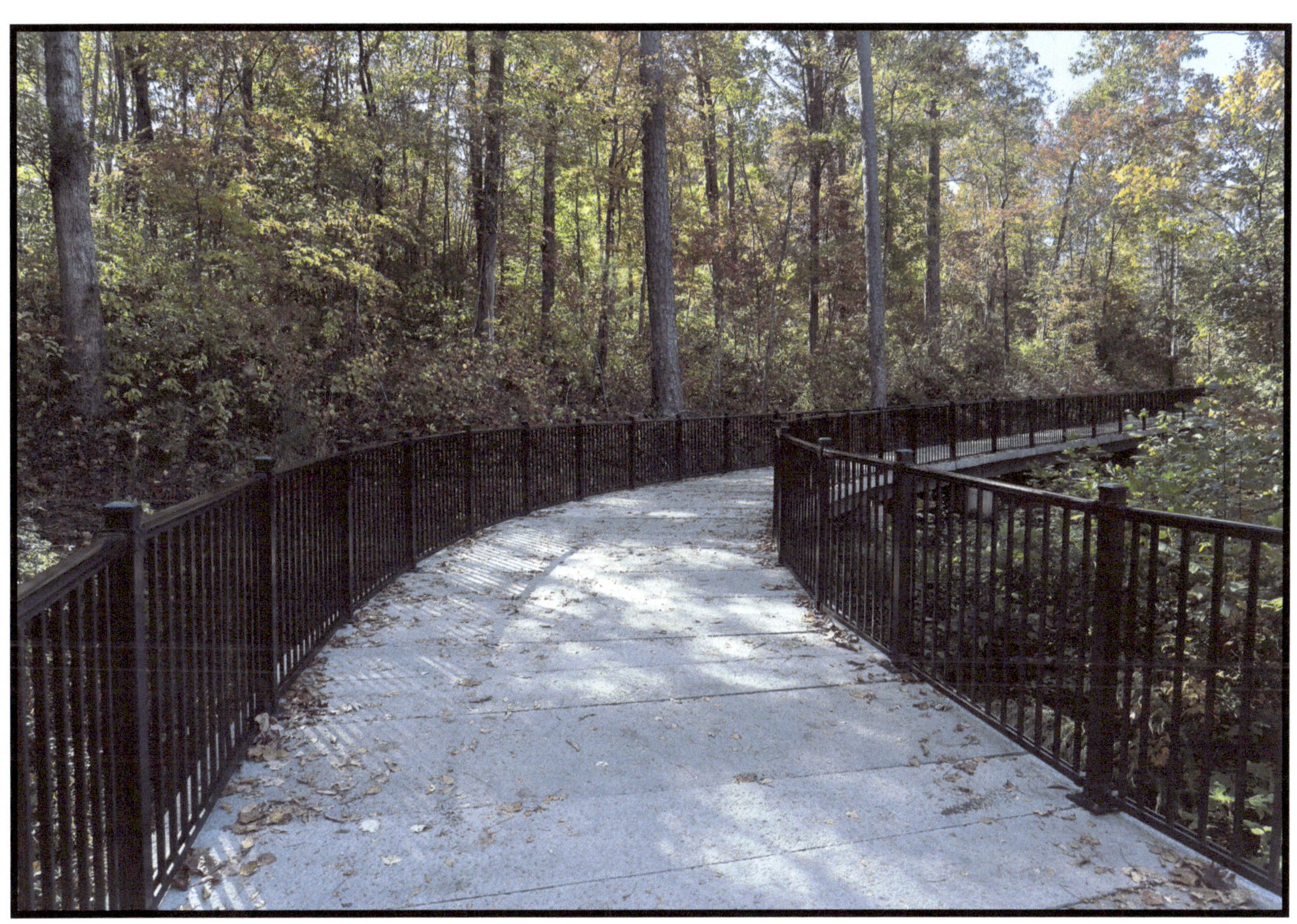

Webwork
(Catawba County, NC)

Porch rail to bush,
fencepost to wire,
trunk to limb,
one limb to another,
across walkways
and wooden steps,
tucked in any concave corner,
interceding between self
and sun, strung up,
glistening with dew,
as taut as life itself.

As long as they exist,
there is no morning you can wake
and find the world
entirely disconnected.

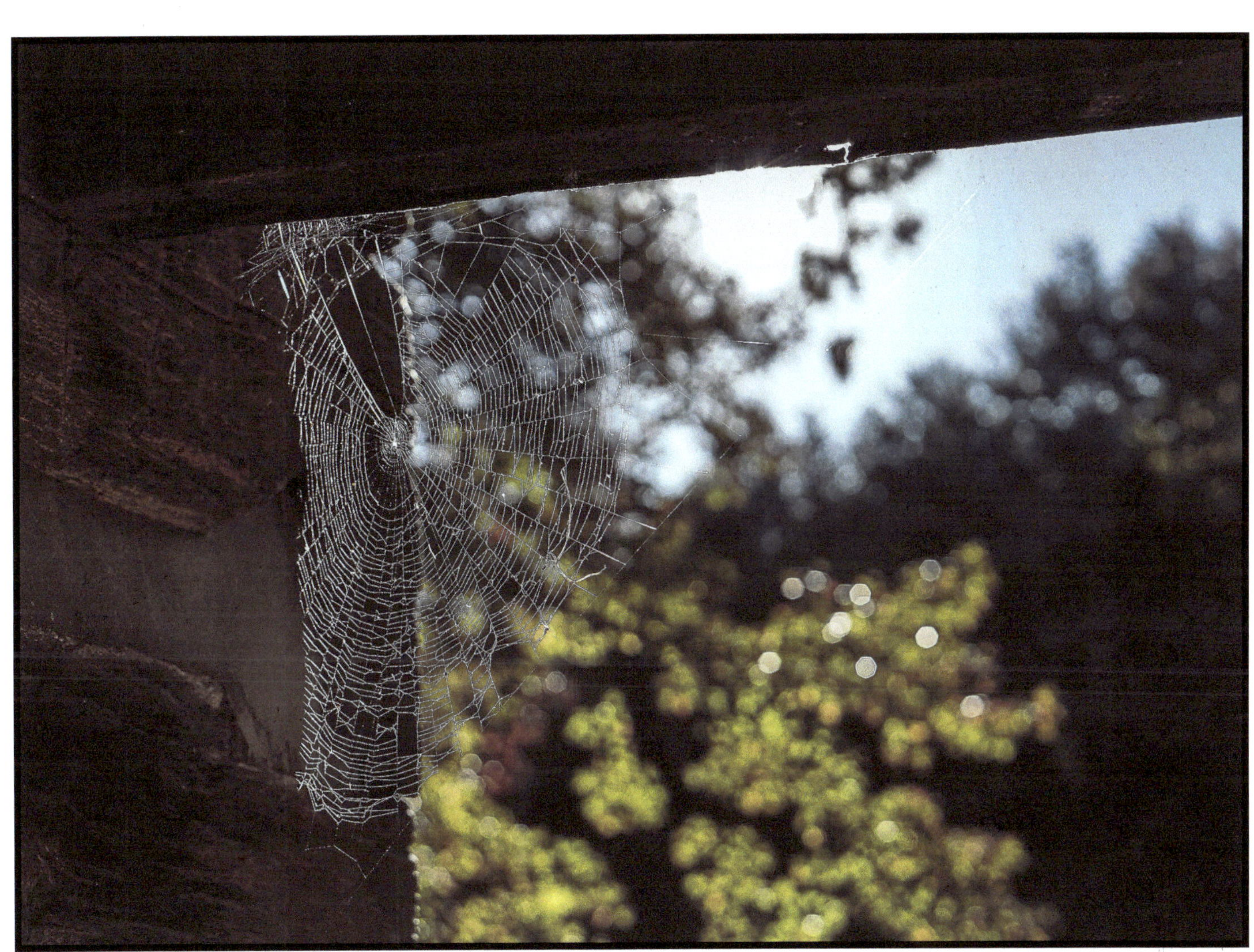

wildflowers blooming
the tractor stops
a moment

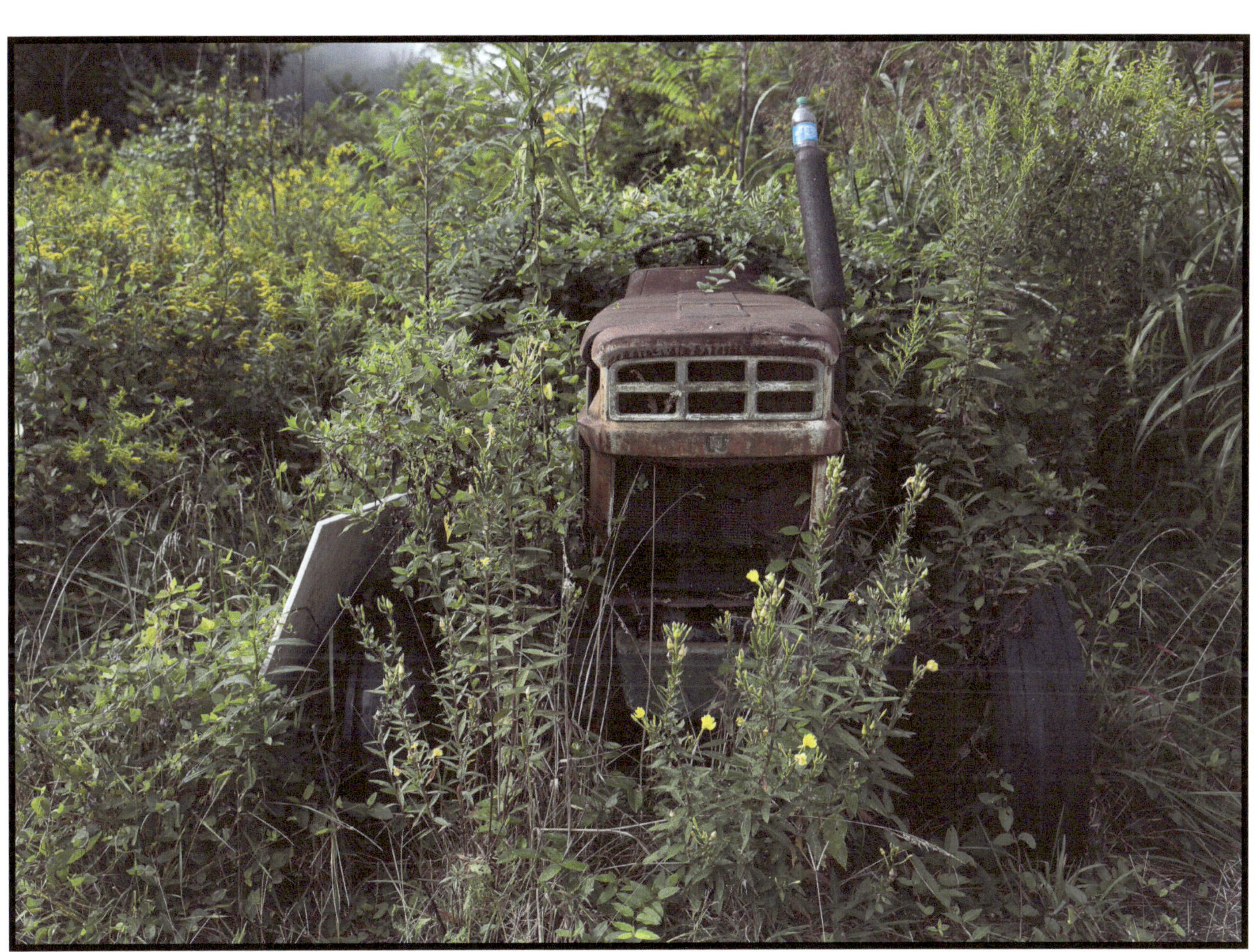

Country Roads
(Catawba County, NC)

Pick a street, any street,
heading out of town
in any direction, north
towards the lake, west
to the mountains, south
across Henry River, east
across the Catawba.
No matter which way you go
you'll be surprised and pleased
at what you might see
Bakers Mountain, Gunpowder Creek
the Icard Dam and Shuford Pond behind it,
Lookout Shoals, Jacobs Fork,
Castle Bridge, Table Rock,
the Brushy Mountains.
And some things unnamed
but nonetheless beautiful,
pastures, and fields,
log cabins, and red barns,
trees and hills,
old houses, old roads,
bridges, birds, and more.
What better way
to spend a day
than riding out
to see what you might find.

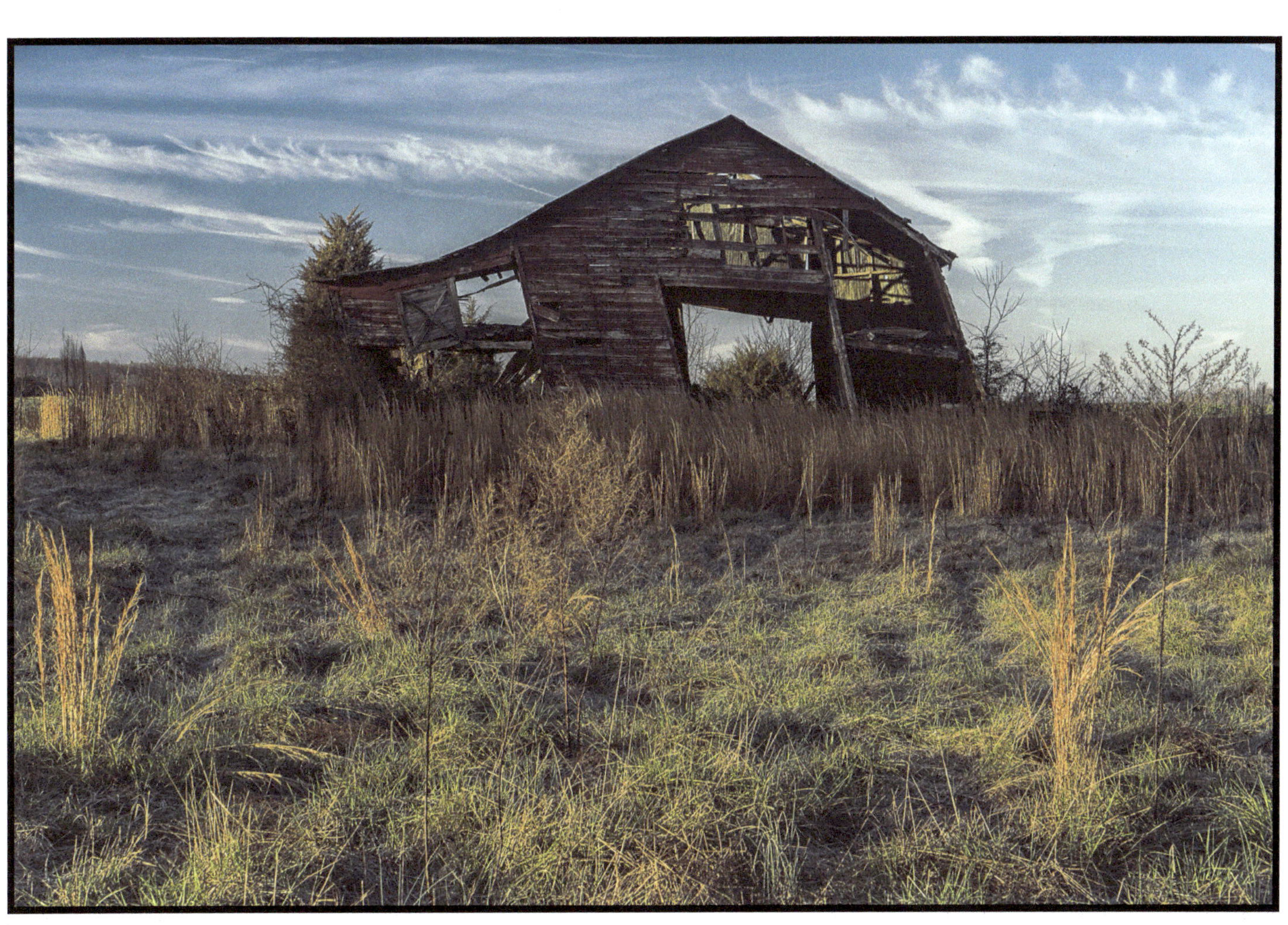

Cicada
(Catawba County, NC)

Not humming or vibrating or buzzing even,
words too small to convey
a sound as big as day.

Strident, ceaseless, maddening,
compression of something called
tymbals, a deforming of the body
as if your ribs collapsed
one at a time and sprang back
300 times a second
causing, maybe a scream,
not from a vocal cord
but from the body itself.

All this to attract a mate
frighten a competitor,
widespread as heat or haze
all defining traits
of Southern summer days.

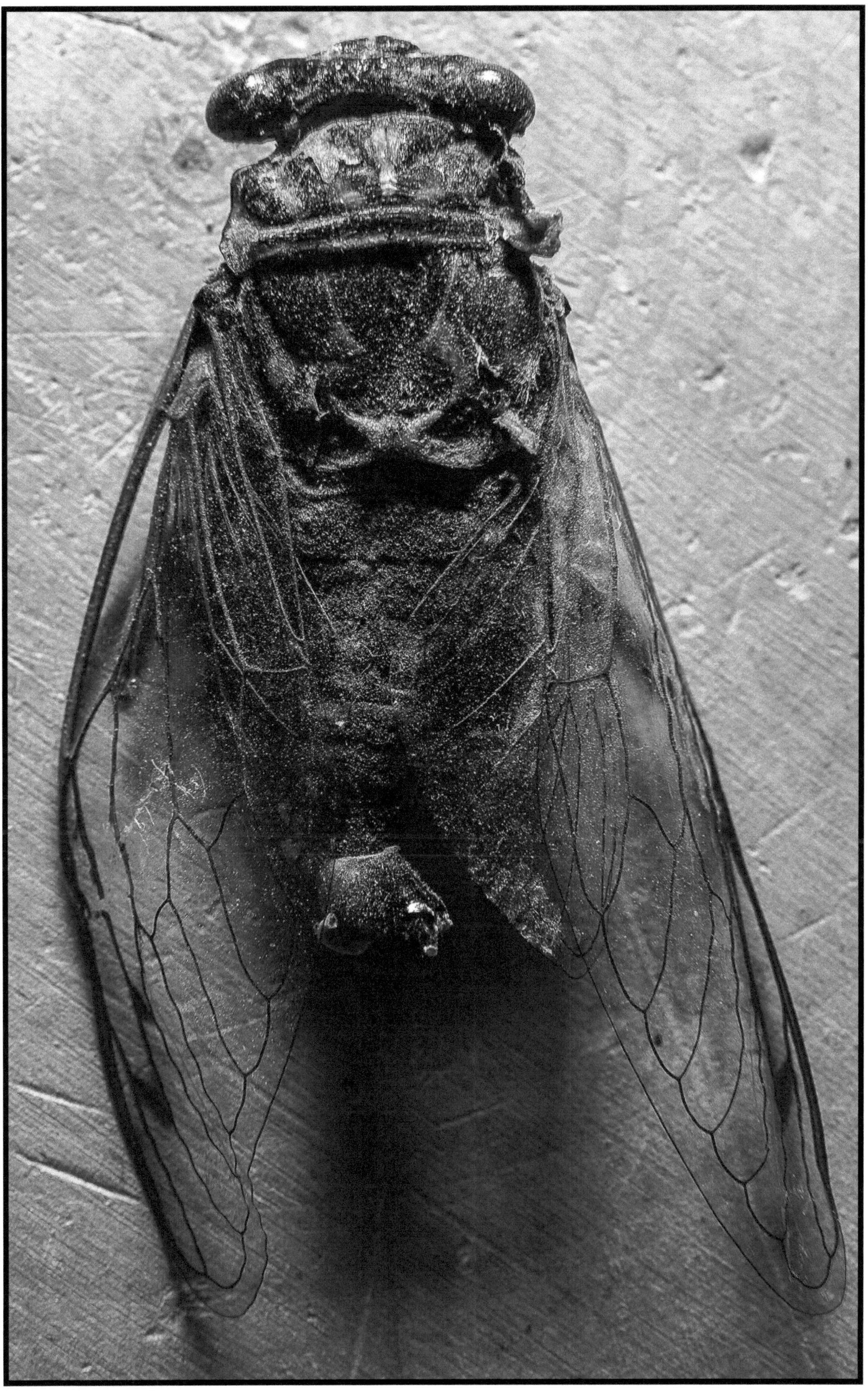

Existential
(Caldwell County, NC)

What is it about a mule
that makes us stop and stare?
To the average eye they are not
unbeautiful, but they lack
the nobility of horses, impressive bulk
of cows, cantankerousness of goats.
Yet there is something in
their imperfections, their curious eyes,
stolid stance, occasional refusal
to tow the line, scant hope
for posterity that seems familiar,
makes us think maybe they
more than any other
stand a chance to understand us.

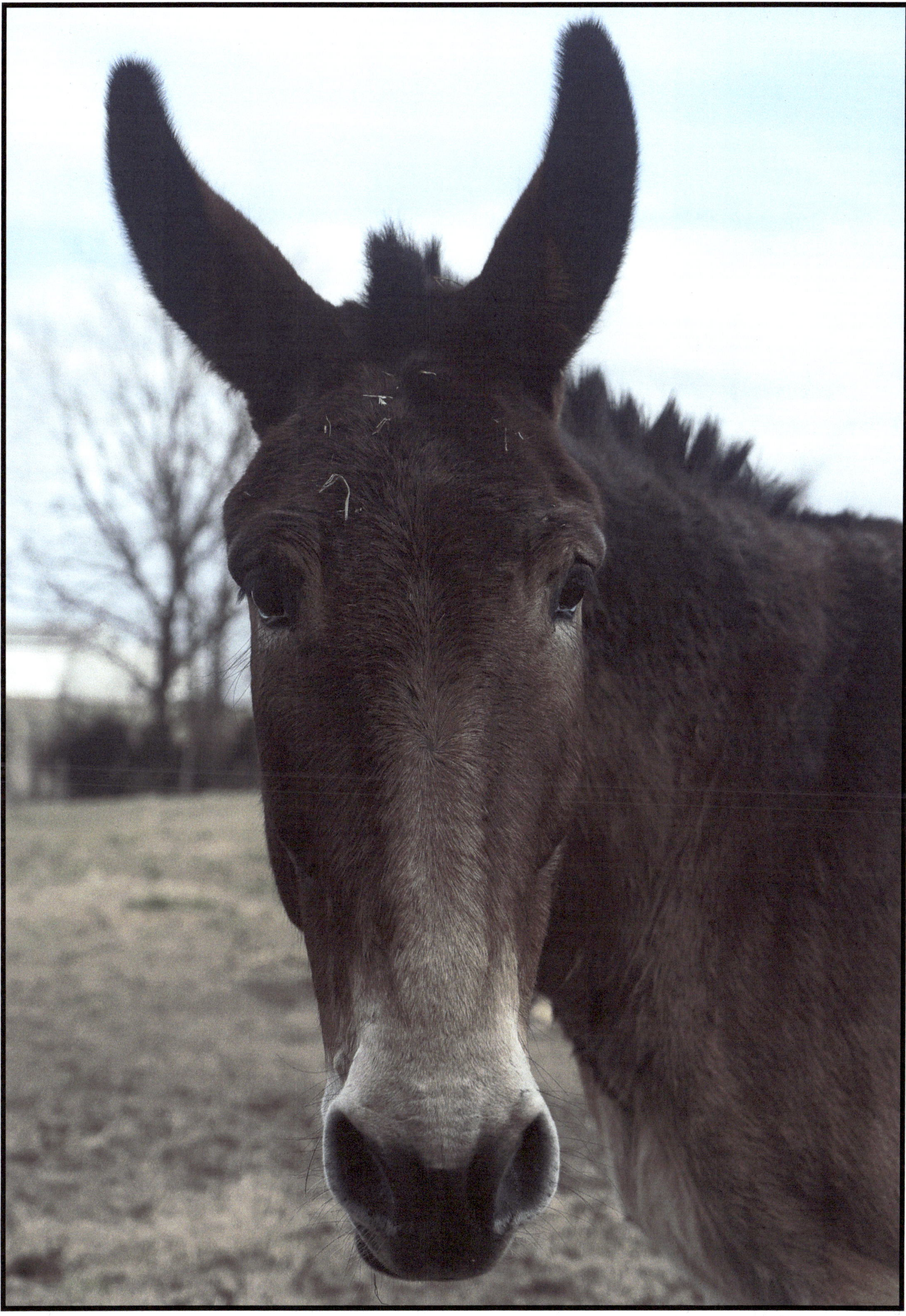

Appaloosa Landscape
(Cleveland County, NC)

In this slow precipitation
of melting snow, the ground
is always wet and putting itself
together like pieces of a puzzle,
here a spot a boot tread,
here another where the sun
shone a bit longer.

Stubborn tufts of grass
shake off what would deny them
room to grow. One world
tumbles down, another rises.

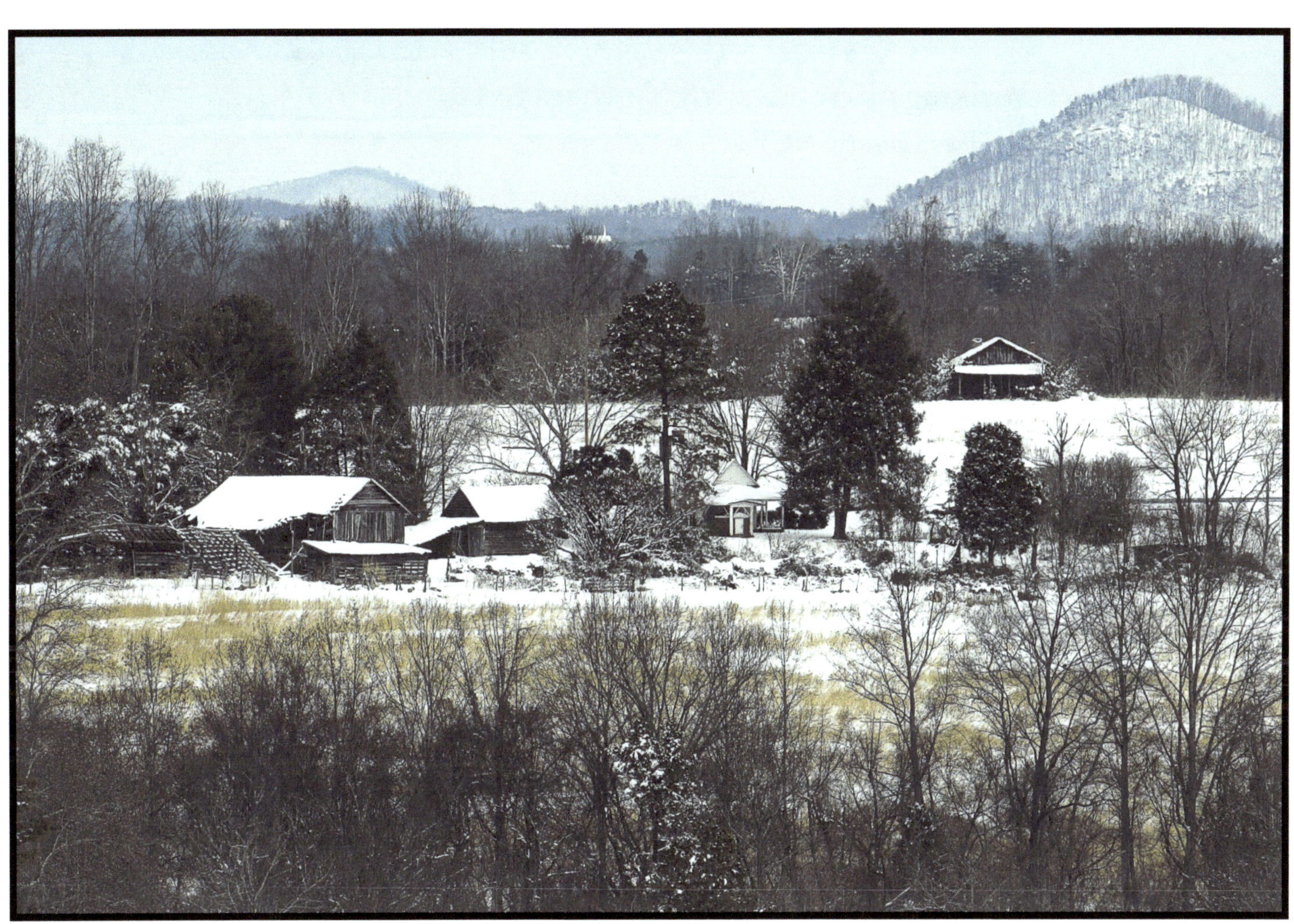

Walking in Woods with Nowhere to Go
(Wilkes County, NC)

There is always another hill to see
over, another trail you have to know
where it goes, a bit of water running
out of sight, a flower shining past
the next path home, a rooftop almost
rising from the ground. There is always
a hint of movement, a light between the trees.
There is always a reason to go further.

You know this will always be yours.
Everything you touch with innocence,
without motive, becomes a part of you.
It feels right to share it with everyone.

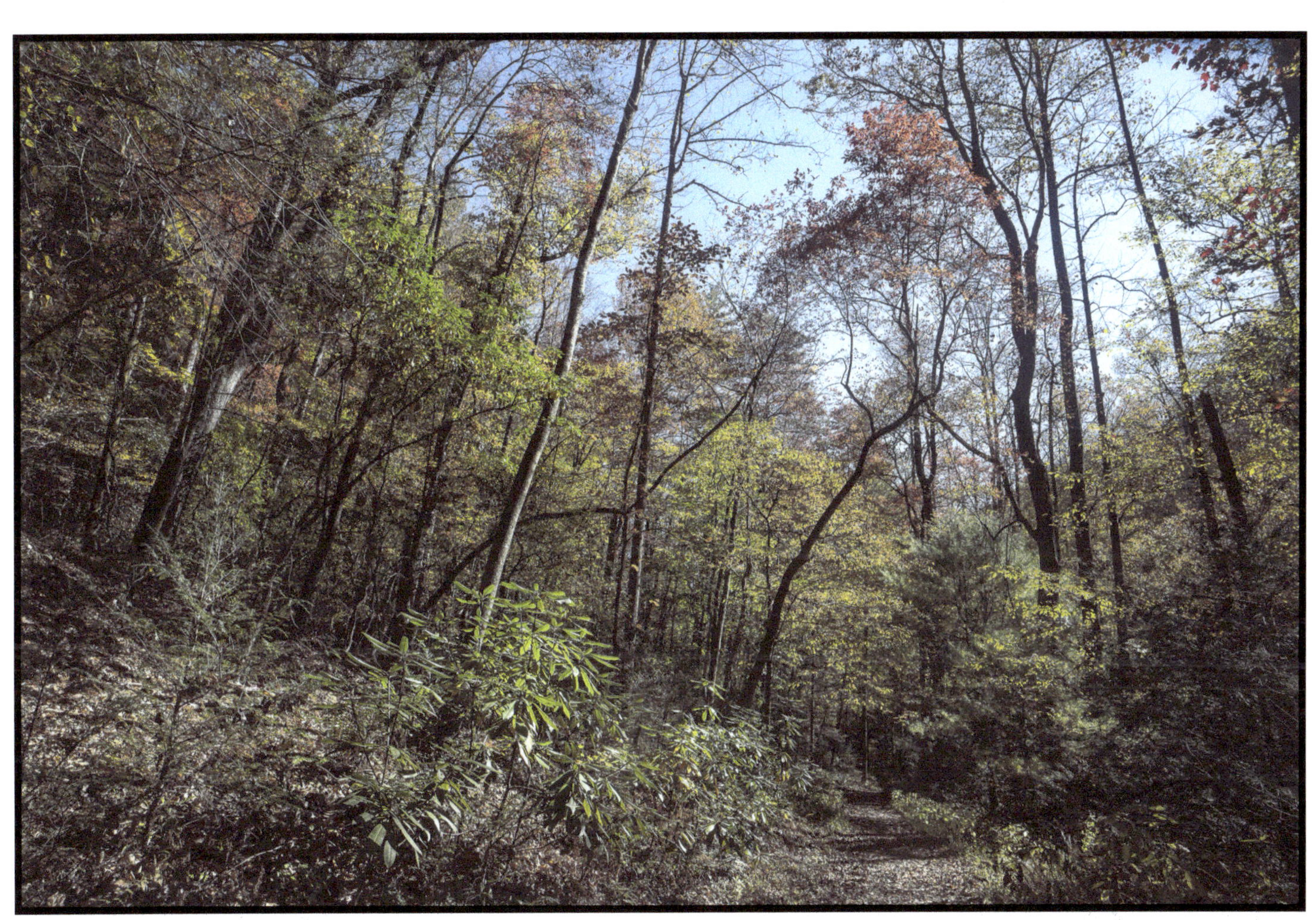

from this rocky perch

blackbird counts twenty peaks

endless blue of sky

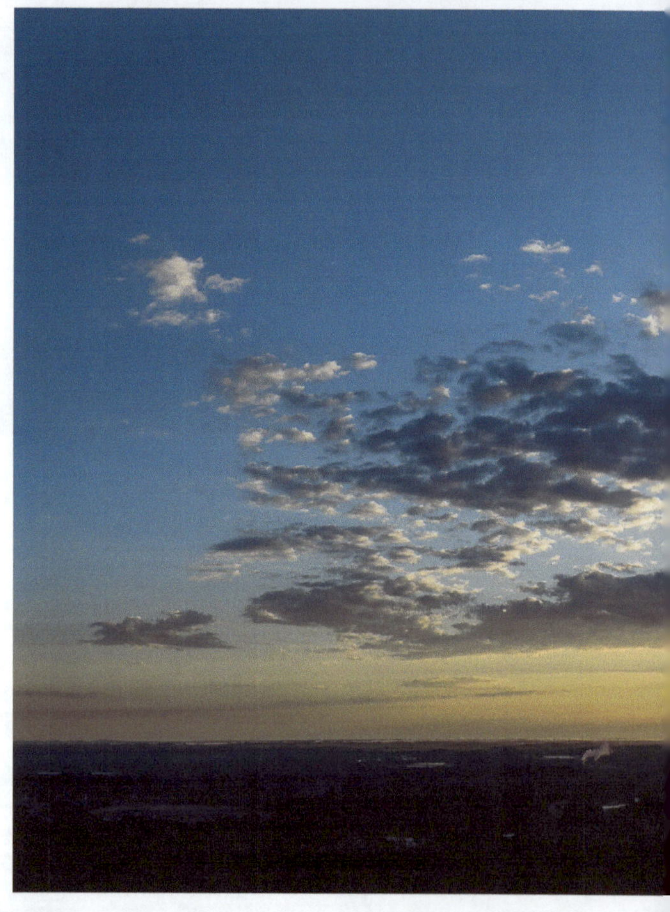

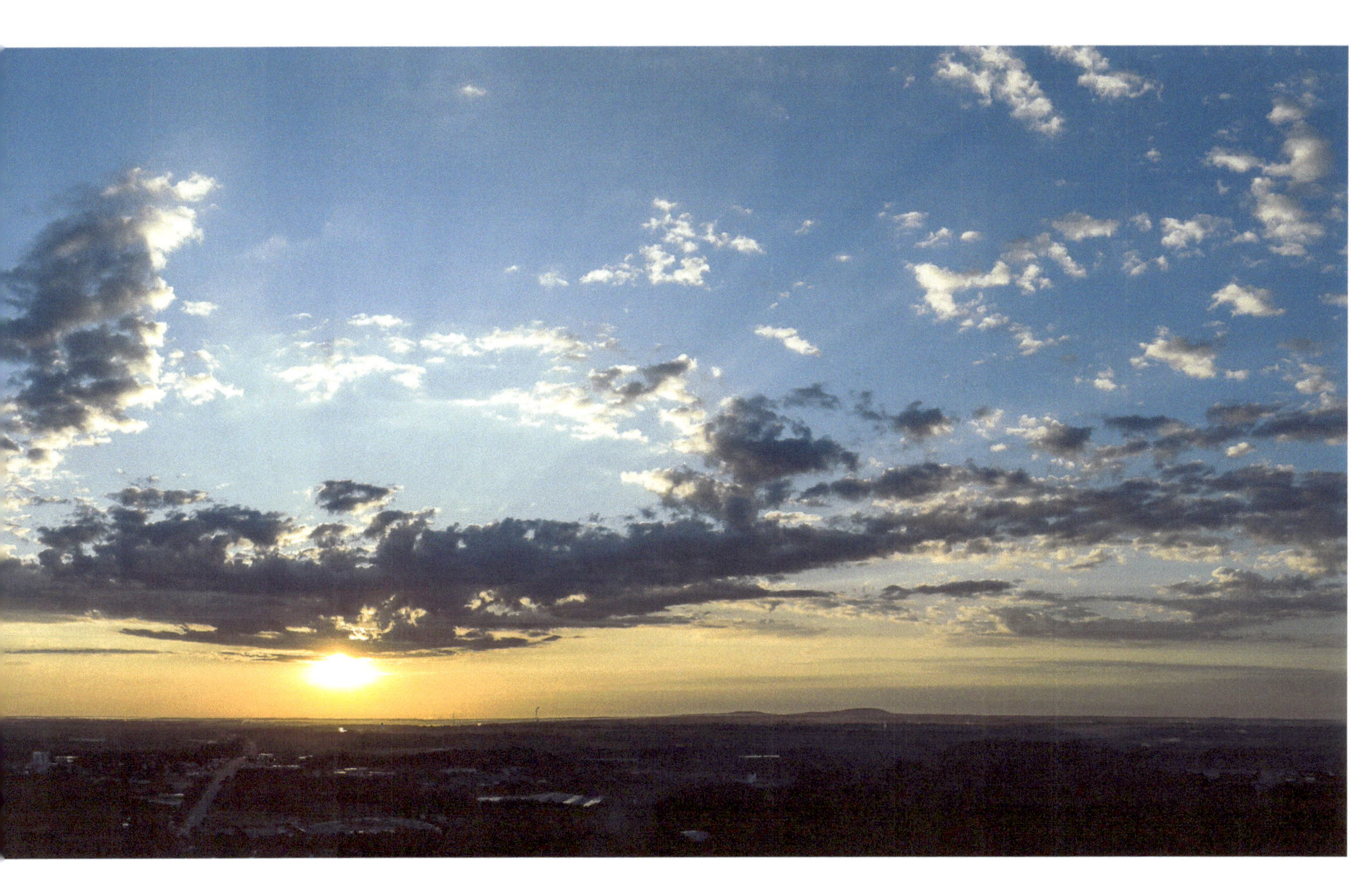

Trees of Hickory
(Catawba County, NC)

From the name you might expect
a proliferation of one kind,
and there are plenty of those
to be sure, but also everywhere you look
are crepe myrtles, giant oaks in Oakwood,
some of the biggest magnolias
you've ever seen, and in gardens,
and parks, back yards, and the arboretum
a variety you'd never imagine
could grow and prosper here:
pomegranates, and eucalyptus,
zelkova and the bee-bee tree
palmetto, ginkgo, and cork tree,
possumhaw and osmanthus,
hemlock, birch and holly,
snowbell and spruce,
witch alder and sourwood,
smoke tree and coffee tree,
pussy willow, linden, and cypress,
sweet gum and Chinese toon,
catalpa, cudrania, and crabapple,
sycamore, hornbeam, and raintree,
mulberry, cherry, and fig,
and of course, shagbark, pignut,
and pecan to name a few.
And though you know the importance
of names, of remembering names,
and calling them out, you've learned
that each tree, like each city, each person
is unique, and no name, no label,
can ever describe it all.

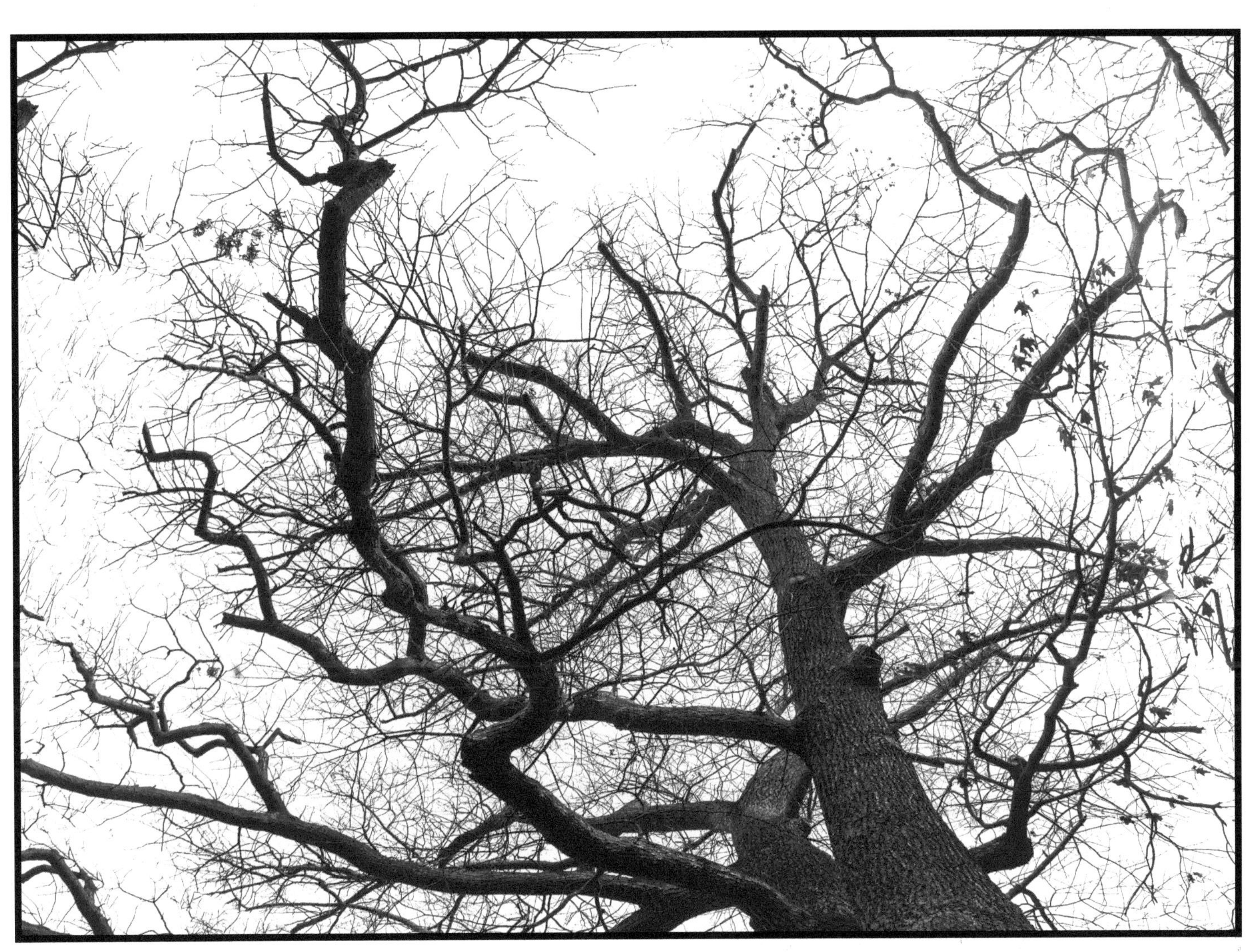

Ineffable

(Burke County, NC)

Though all he has are words, he keeps trying
to wrap his mind around the things he sees,
hawk's hover, sunrise, stars appearing
one by one, crocuses rising through snow,
cherry trees popping open on a single day,
mesmerizing dance of fire, water falling
over rock, the beauty of space between the trees
in woods, the filigree of leafless limbs
filling a winter sky, the sight of the perfect
stone skipping beyond his ability to count,
the fact that even though all he has
are words, he keeps trying anyway.

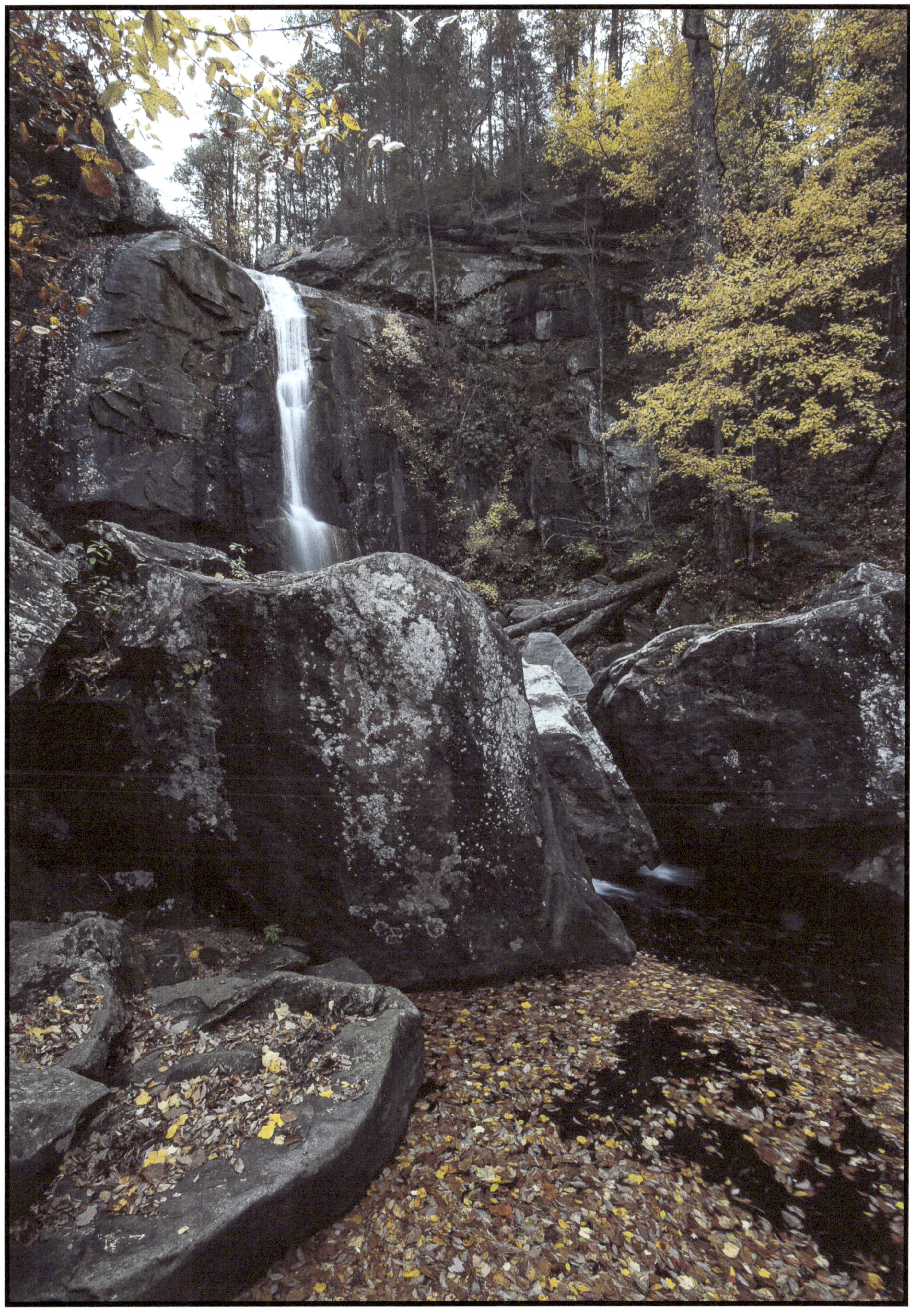

Looking for Faces in the Night Sky
(Catawba County, NC)

These are things anyone could have made
up. The stars are nothing but stars,
and playing dot-to-dot in the night
sky makes anything possible.
Years ago from the stone porch
my grandfather pointed them out:
the lion, the great bear, the hunter's sword.
This one he called Mary and showed me
how the stars made a woman's face.

Looking for faces in the night sky
we string stars into shapes of things
we fear or long to remember.
I see spider, sparrowhawk, bobwhite.
This one I'll call woman becoming
an angel, the grotesque buds of wings
sprouting in her back.

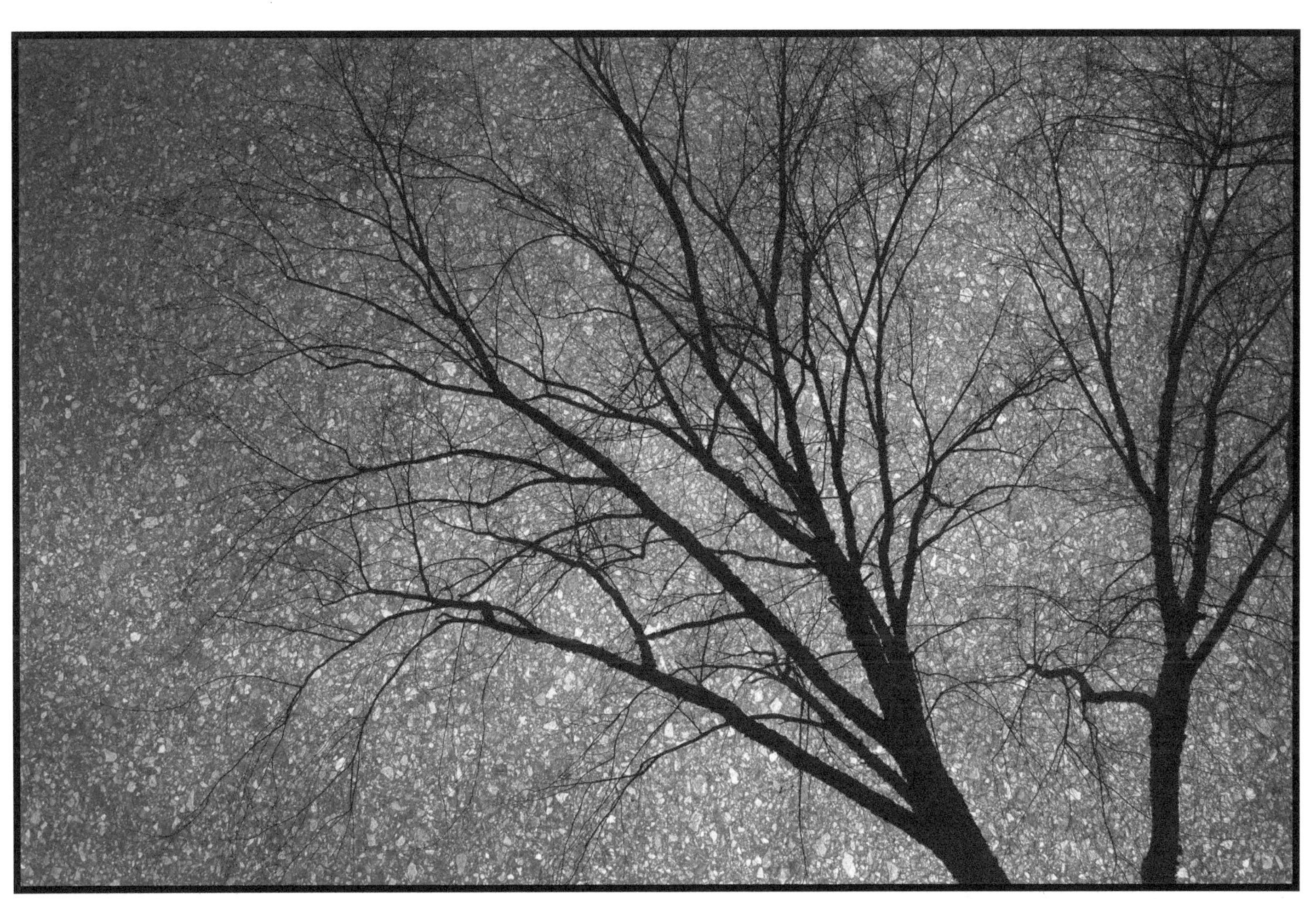

Through

(Catawba County, NC)

The old oak
has lost
more leaves
than most
has learned
to let
more light
shine through

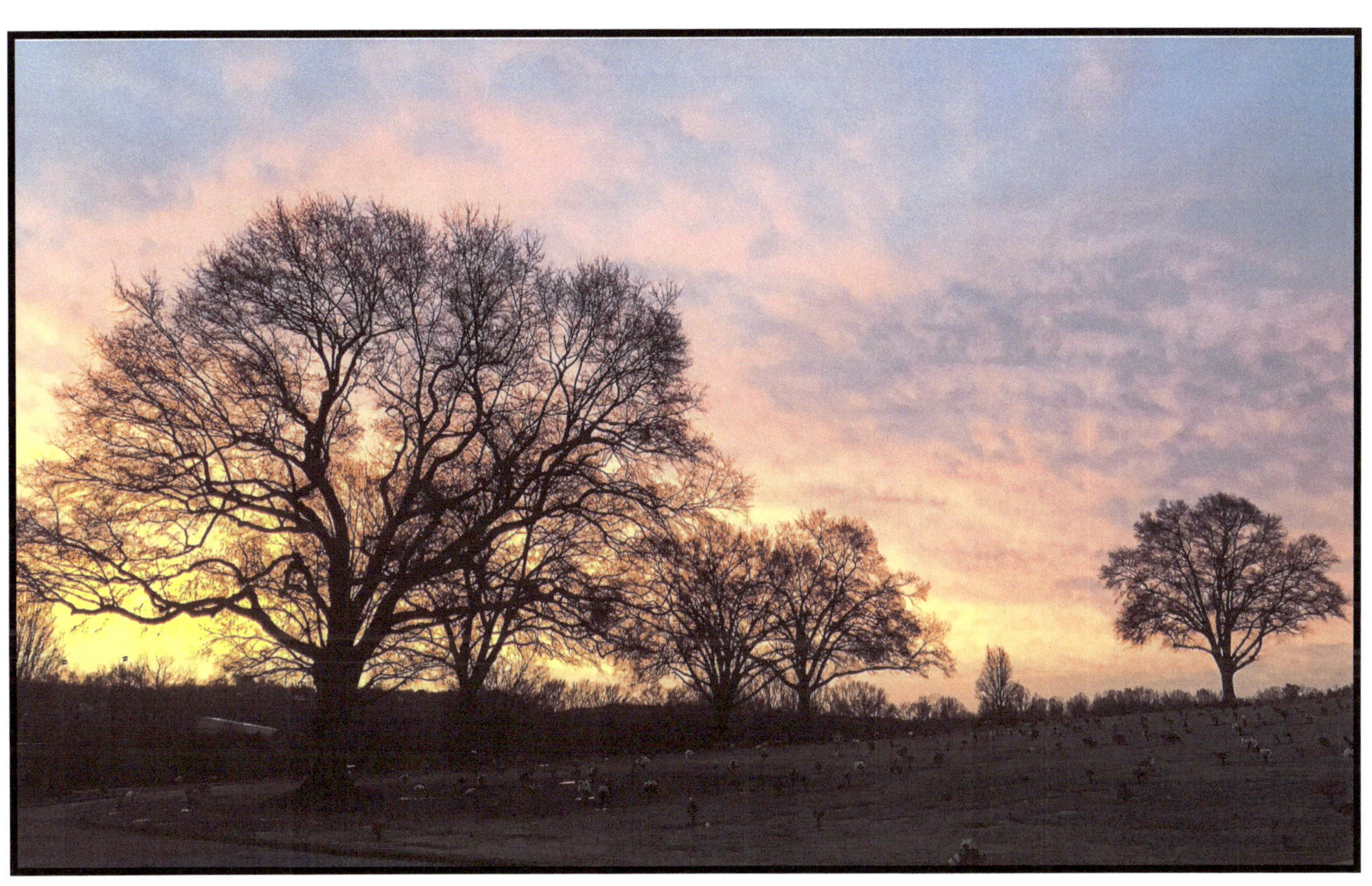

It's the View
(Catawba County, NC)

Mountain View,
Longview,
Viewmont,
Ridgeview,
every little town
or part of town
around here
seems named
after the view,
and it's true
that looking west
any morning
fills your vision
with a panorama
of peaks to be ascended,
with dreams of the Blue Ridge
rising out of the dark,
and any evening
with broad bands
of red setting
softly behind
misty mountains,
with the comfort
of some place called home.
For more than 250 years
and probably longer,
this view has been appreciated,
as if even the sky
knew our days
and nights would always
be better if begun
with a view of mountains.

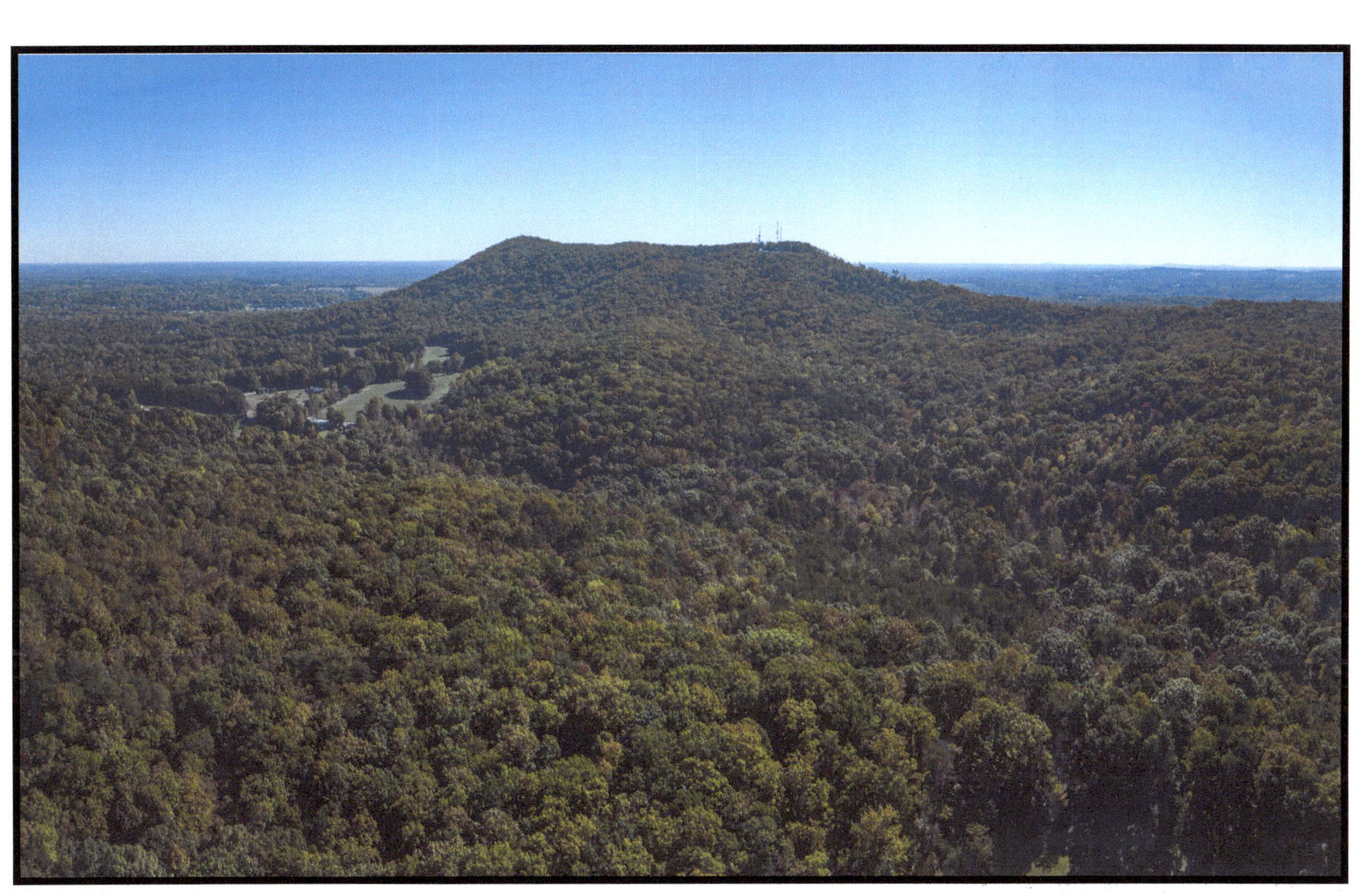

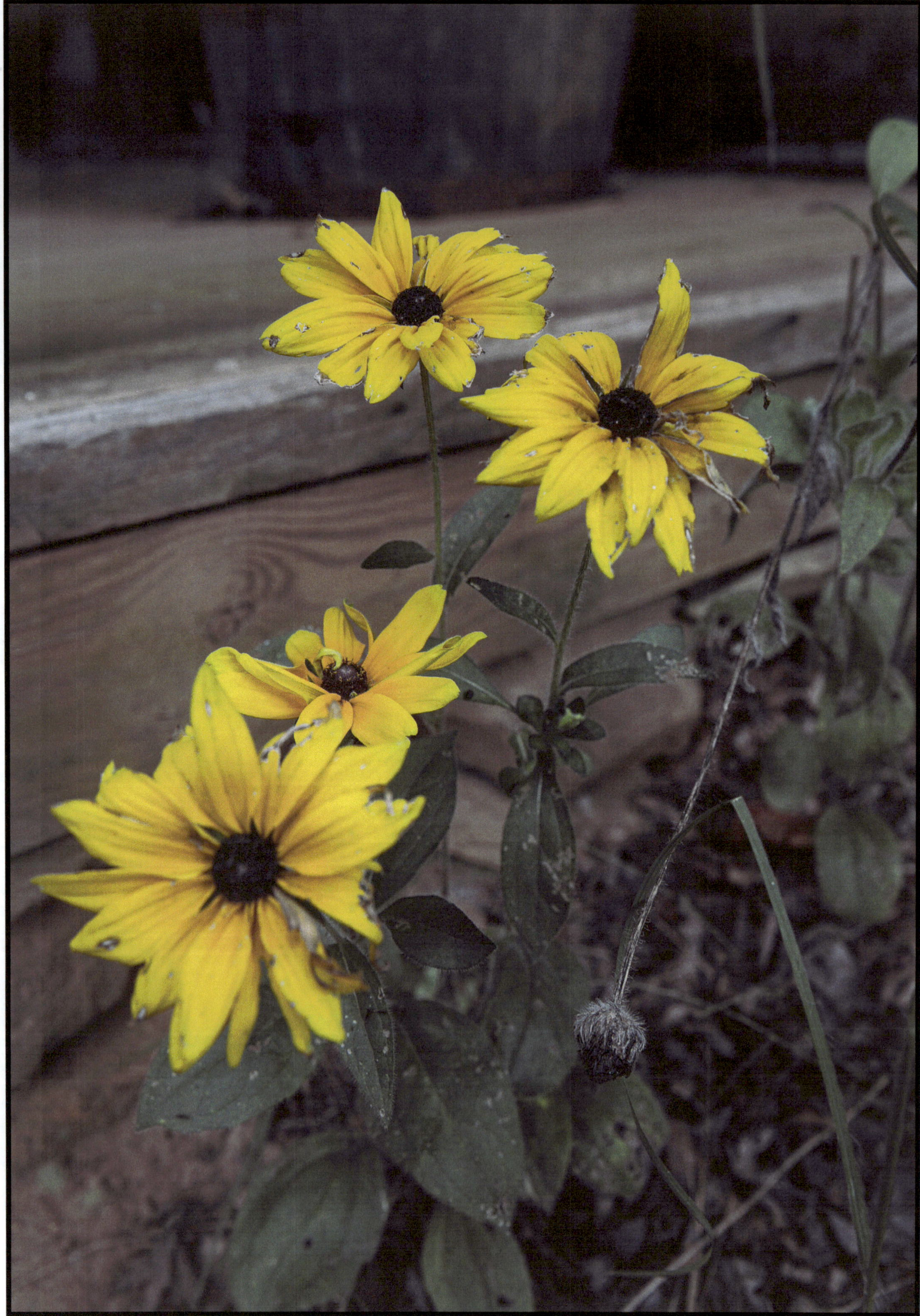

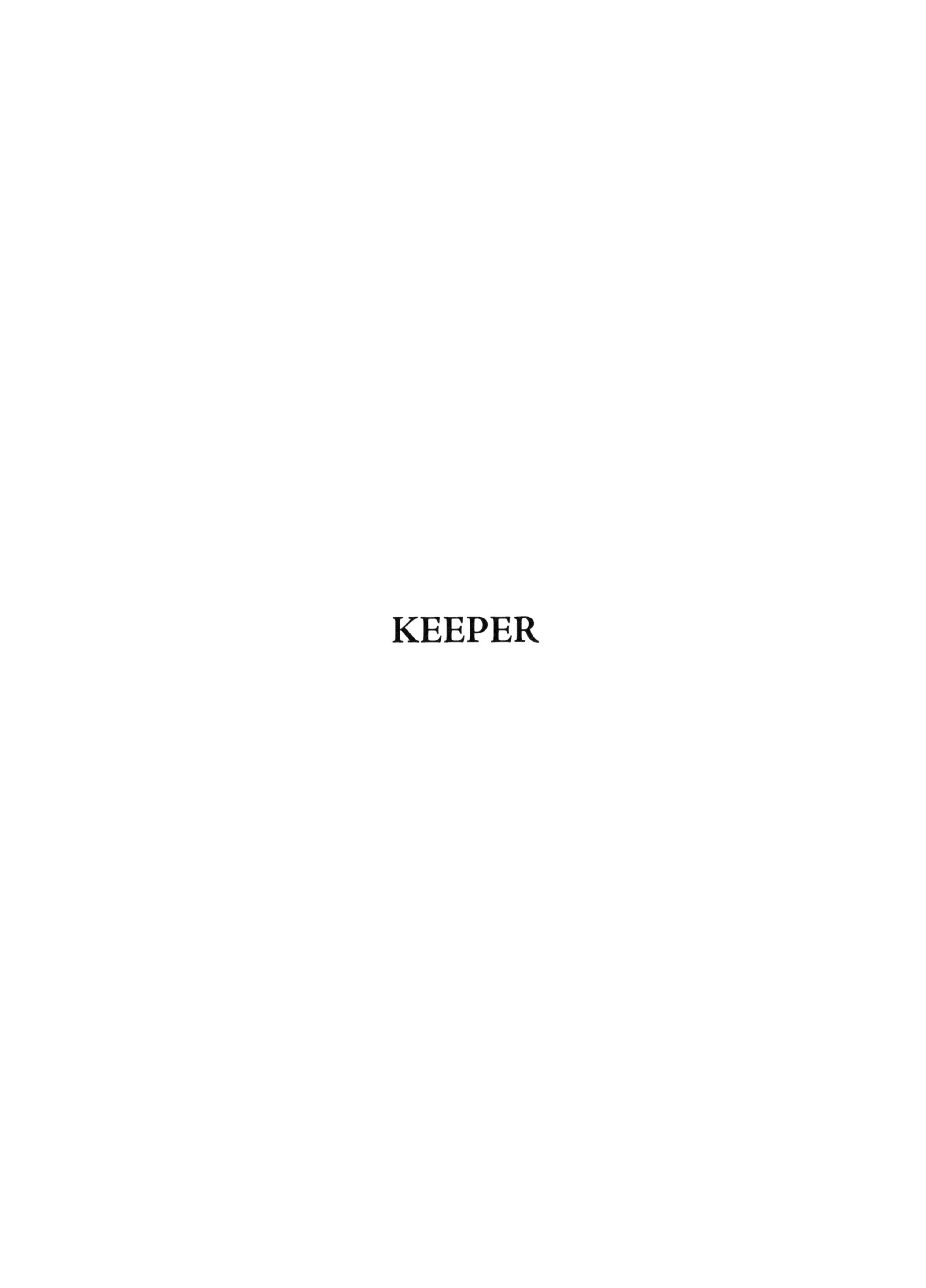

KEEPER

Something That Loves a Wall

(Catawba County, NC)

All the rage lately, becoming
as common as churches, or Dollar Generals,
creating a sense of community,
stories and images we share together,
a touchstone for art and ideas, a place
connecting past, present, future.
Some are about history, Piedmont Wagon,
the Miracle of Hickory, Ellis Mill;
some about beauty, luscious lilies,
roses, horses breaking free;
some make statements, hands joined,
black and white working together;
some welcome you to Hickory,
blue skies, green trees, a kayak on the lake;
some are just about fun, a rain shower
and a fixed umbrella you stand under,
a door where there could be a door
but there isn't, a window where there could be
a window, but there isn't, and a girl
hanging out the window above the bicycle
she might have ridden home on;
but wherever you go there's one or another
to attract your eye, invite you to look,
think, laugh, remember, or just admire.

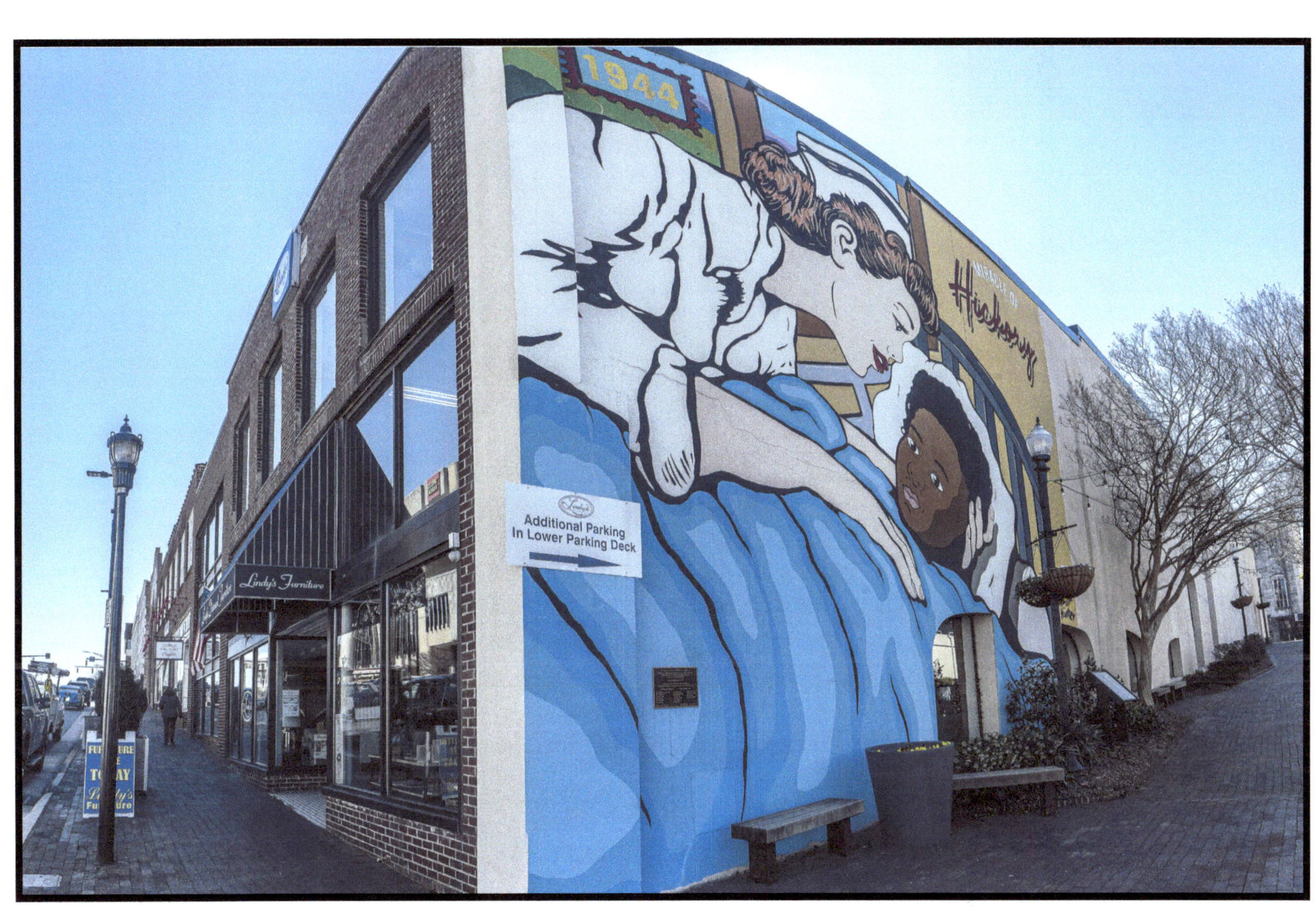
1944
MIRACLE OF
Hickory
Additional Parking
In Lower Parking Deck
Lindy's Furniture

Found Poem, Hickory Daily Record, 12/14/2022
(Catawba County, NC)

Baby Jesus Stolen from Church!,
just taken in broad daylight,
or maybe at night, (no one knows
for sure), along with a camel and a sheep,
ten feet in all, three lives,
useful for travel and warmth
among other possibilities.
No one heard any crying or bleating;
there was no sign of a struggle;
no prints were left on anything that remained:
a manger, Mary and Joseph, wise men, more sheep.
It was, it seems, an immaculate theft.
A deacon of the church discovered Jesus
missing when he arrived on Thursday morning.
He first noticed the livestock were gone,
and looking, realized there was no Jesus.
Jesus is estimated to be worth $450,
the camel and sheep a bit more.
Research reveals it's not the first time
Jesus has been stolen, always returned,
miraculously, by Christmas Eve.
Mary, Joseph, and the wise men
have been removed out of fear
that they might be taken as well.
The chief of police says it would be nice
if whoever stole them would just return them,
preferably before another miracle is needed.

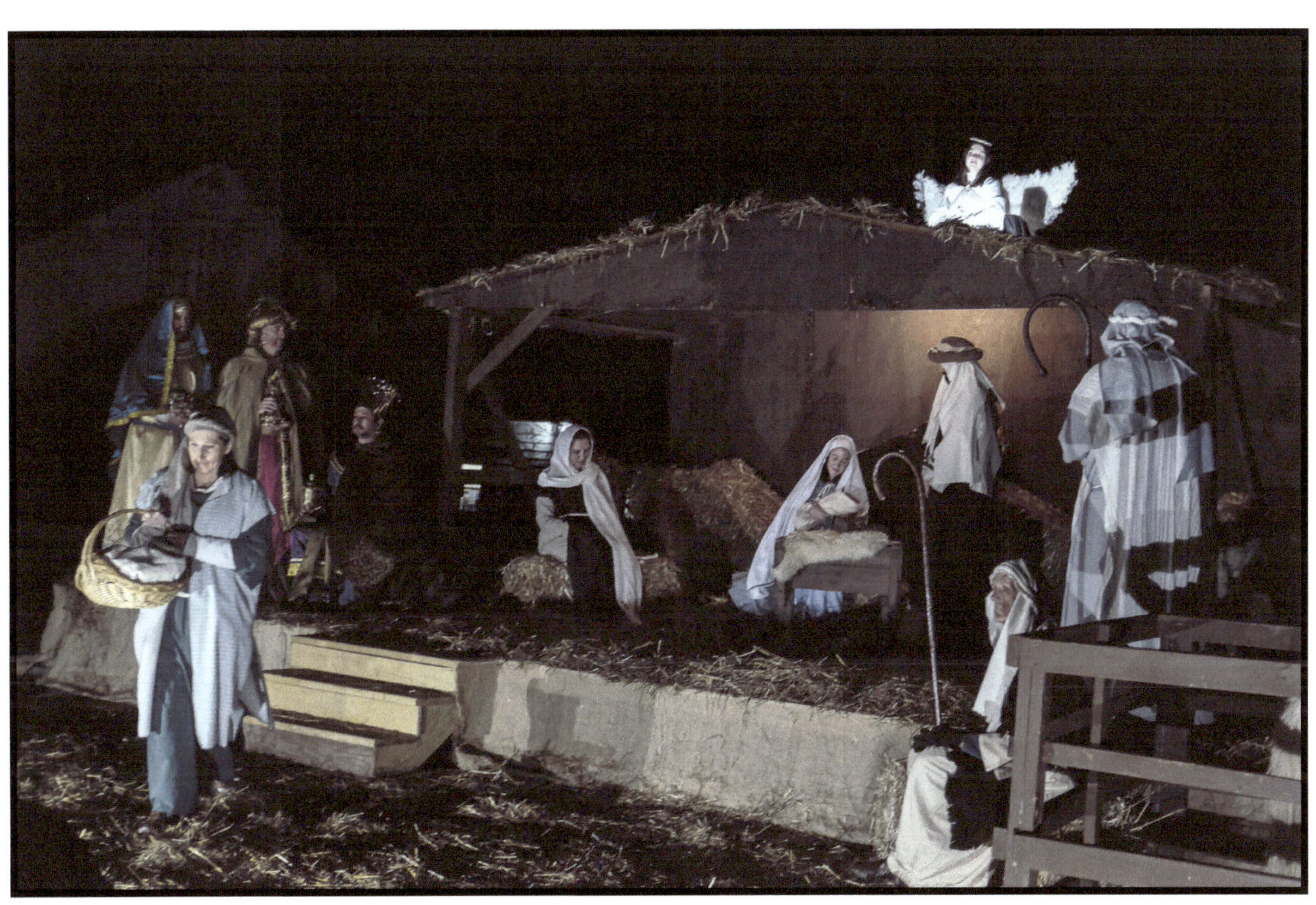

Remembering Blue
(Cleveland County, NC)

Blue was always her favorite color,
cornflower and daisy, crocus and bouncing bet.
She remembers her mother's dishes, cobalt
blue glass, the hood of her father's
Ford Fairlane. She remembers the ceiling
of the front porch summer afternoons,
lying back on the swing, roll of sky
captured in painted slats of blue. She made
a blue garden for shade, columbine,
iris, bellflower and forget-me-nots.
Even music they called the blues, lonely
and familiar, dripping like evening in her mind,
soft and slow and always a little bit sad.
Heaven for her would be like this,
a field full of flowers, ubiquity of blue.

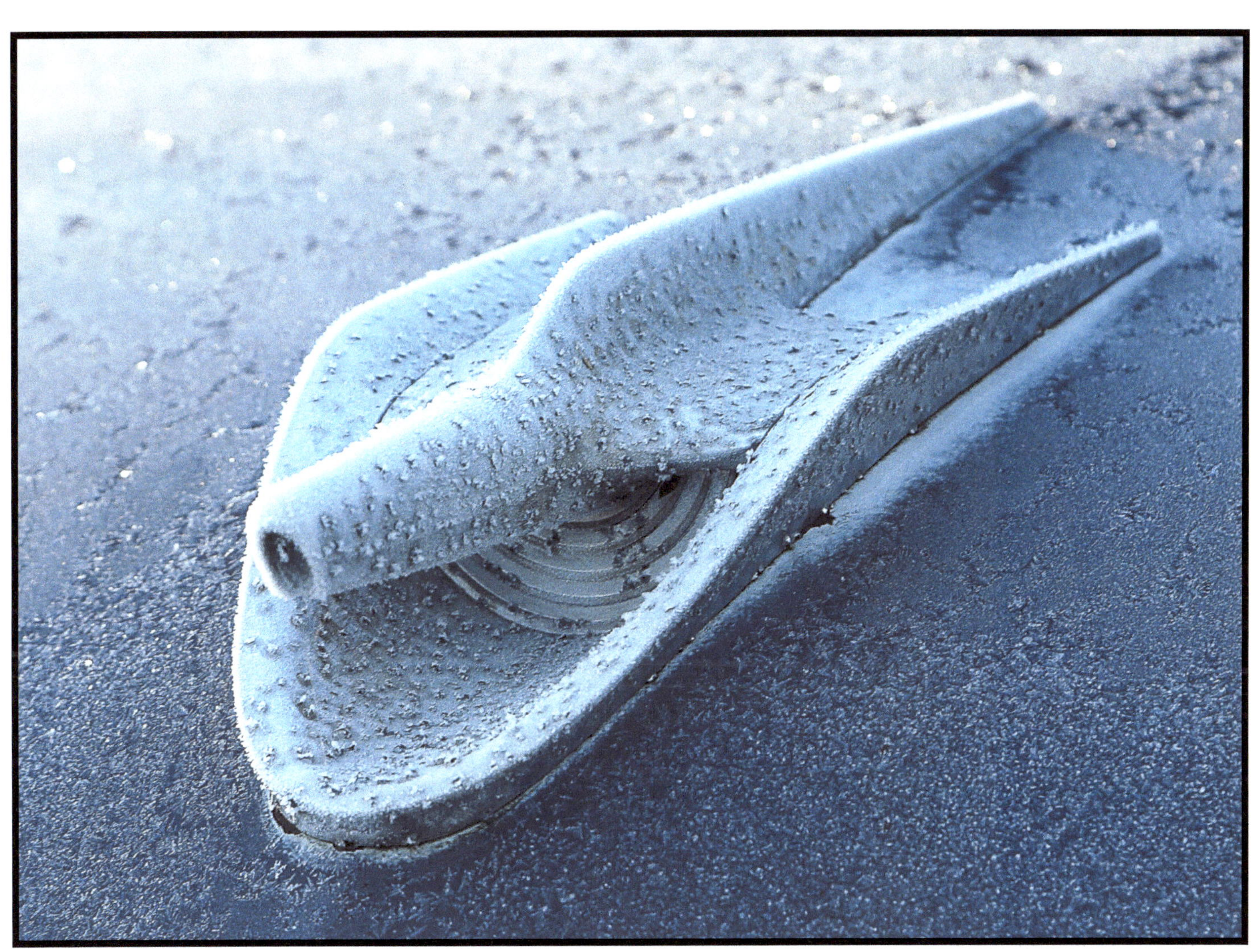

Happy Valley
(Caldwell County, NC)

Small and white,
almost unnoticed,
the chapel sits
against the enormity
of mountain
like a prayer
against the enormity
of time,
just as small,
just as persistent.

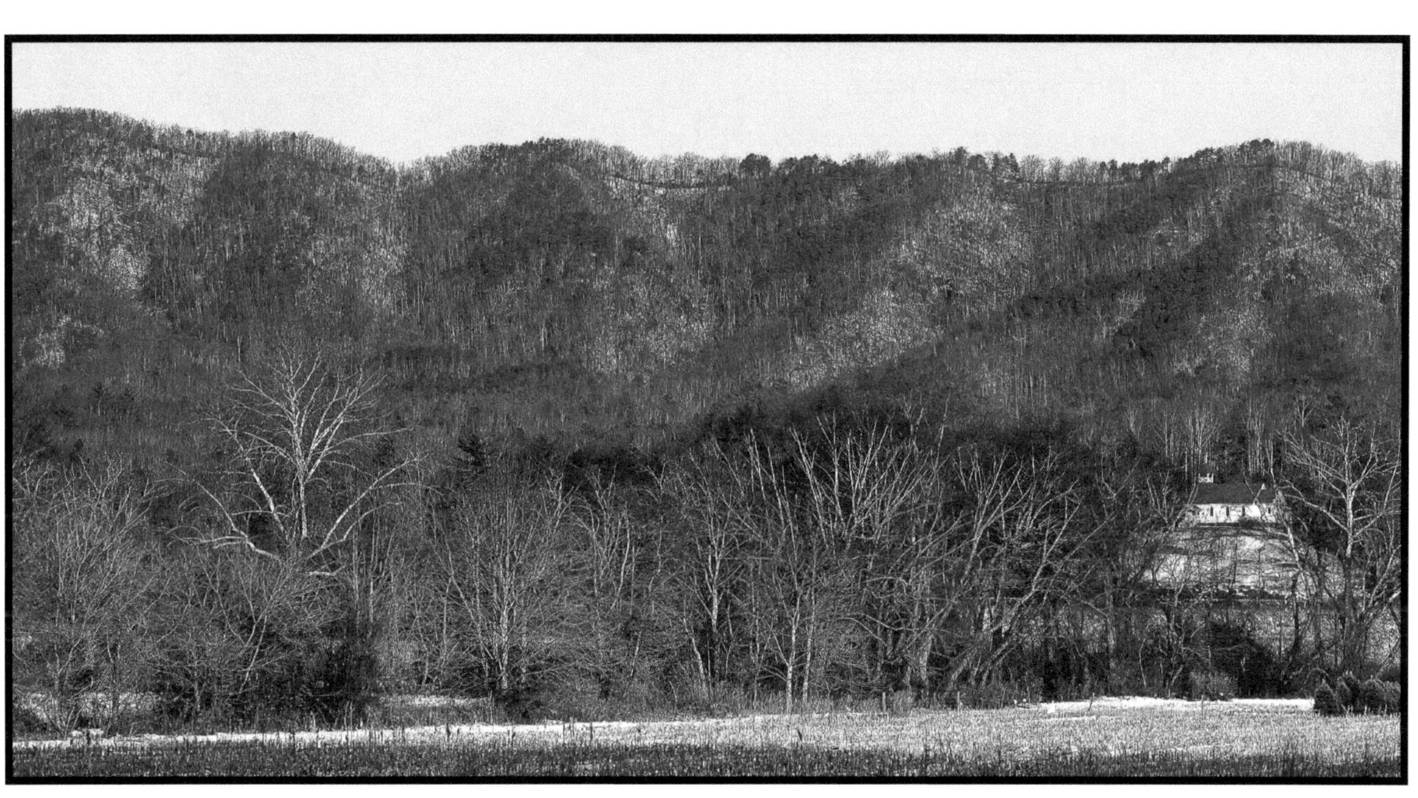

Keeper
(Catawba County, NC)

Heel on shoulder,
hands gripping the shaft,
shift weight forward,
press down,
thin roots popping
as the blade moves through
lean back,
lift.

A hole the only thing it makes,
absence, empty space,
and yet without it, nothing grows,
necessity the smallest understand.

Most come here not to die
but simply to be dead.
Precious few come to live
and do the work
of keeping things going.

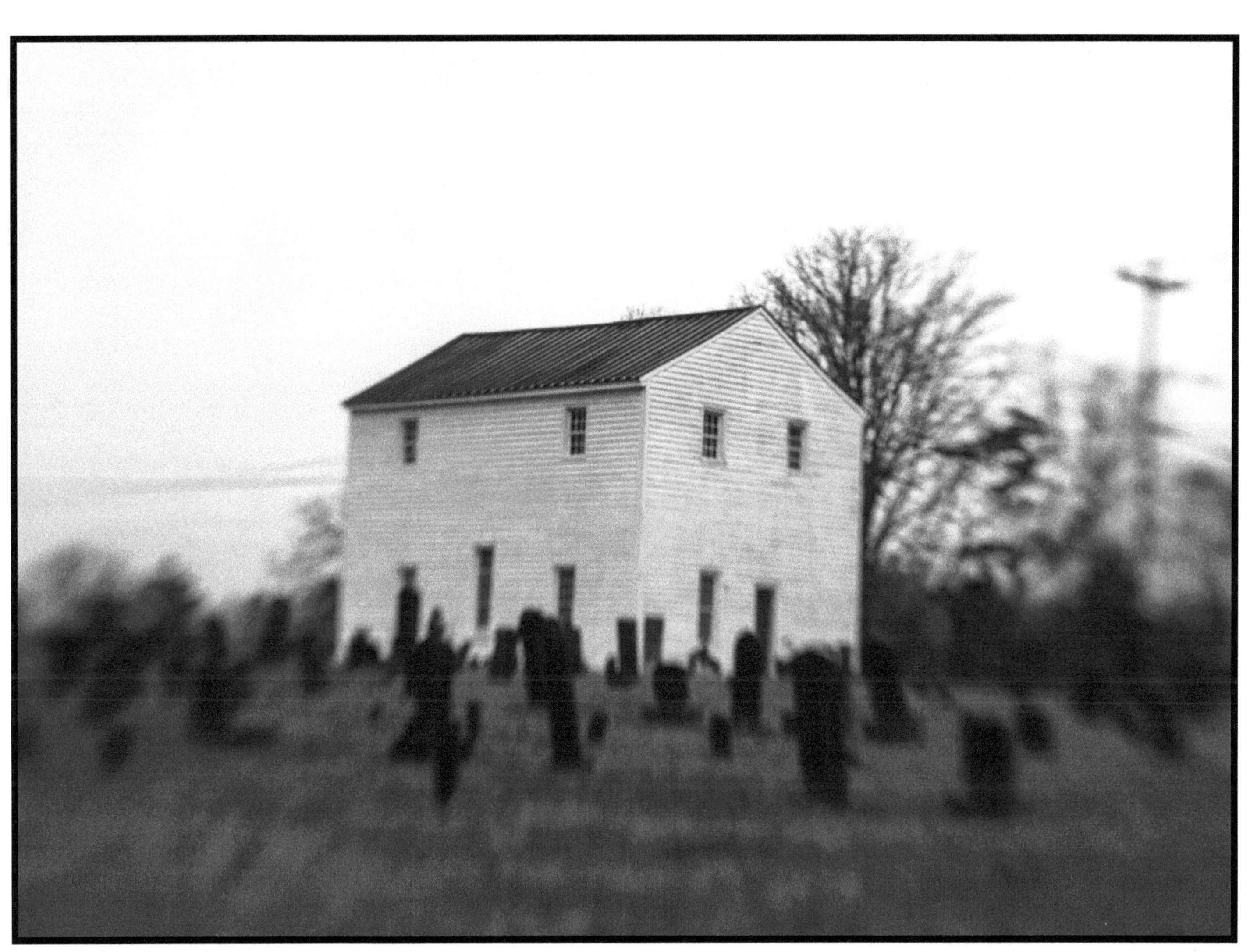

A Gift of Water

(Catawba County, NC)

The moon shines like always.
There's nothing new about
its blue light on white
stones in a night grown
bright with flowers.

It is not a quiet night.
The weeds are wailing
and gnashing their teeth.
The willows are wringing
their hands and tearing

their hair. Like always,
the stones are beating
their breasts, their hardened words
crying out from the dead
town, the town of boxes.

These mounds will never be quiet.
They chitter in the fog
like leaves, longing for life,
or freedom, for transportation,
a time wet with worms.

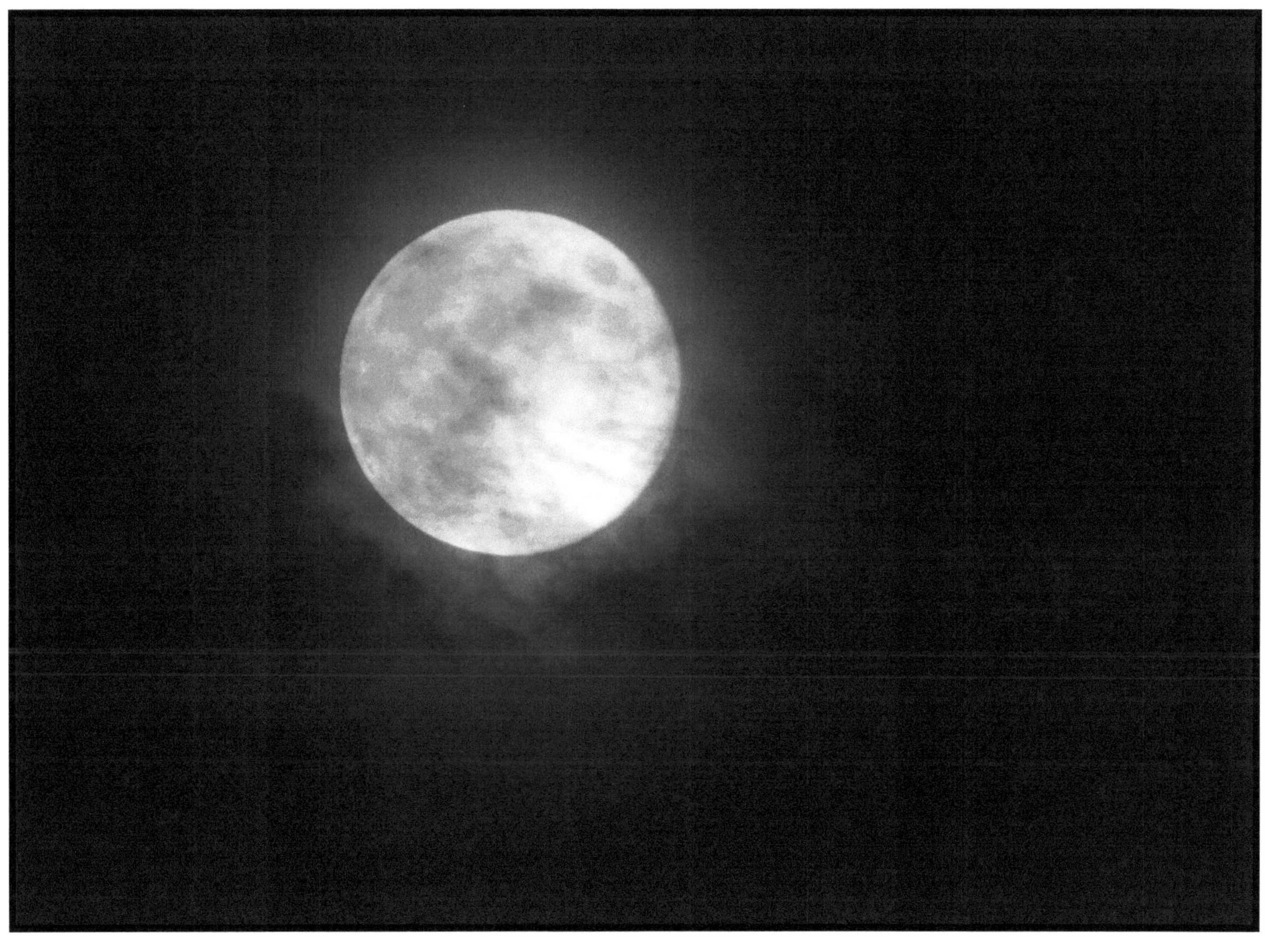

Hickory, 2023
(Catawba County, NC)

Named for a tree,
not a kind of tree,
a particular tree,
a hickory, of course,
shading a particular tavern,
a resting spot really
for people going
somewhere else
built on what was
an intersection
for stagecoach,
native travelers
on native trails
before it was anything
else except wilderness,
and now, a new awareness
of green space,
and it becomes again
Hickory Trail,
City Walk,
River Walk,
a place made
for bringing people
not to somewhere else
but together.

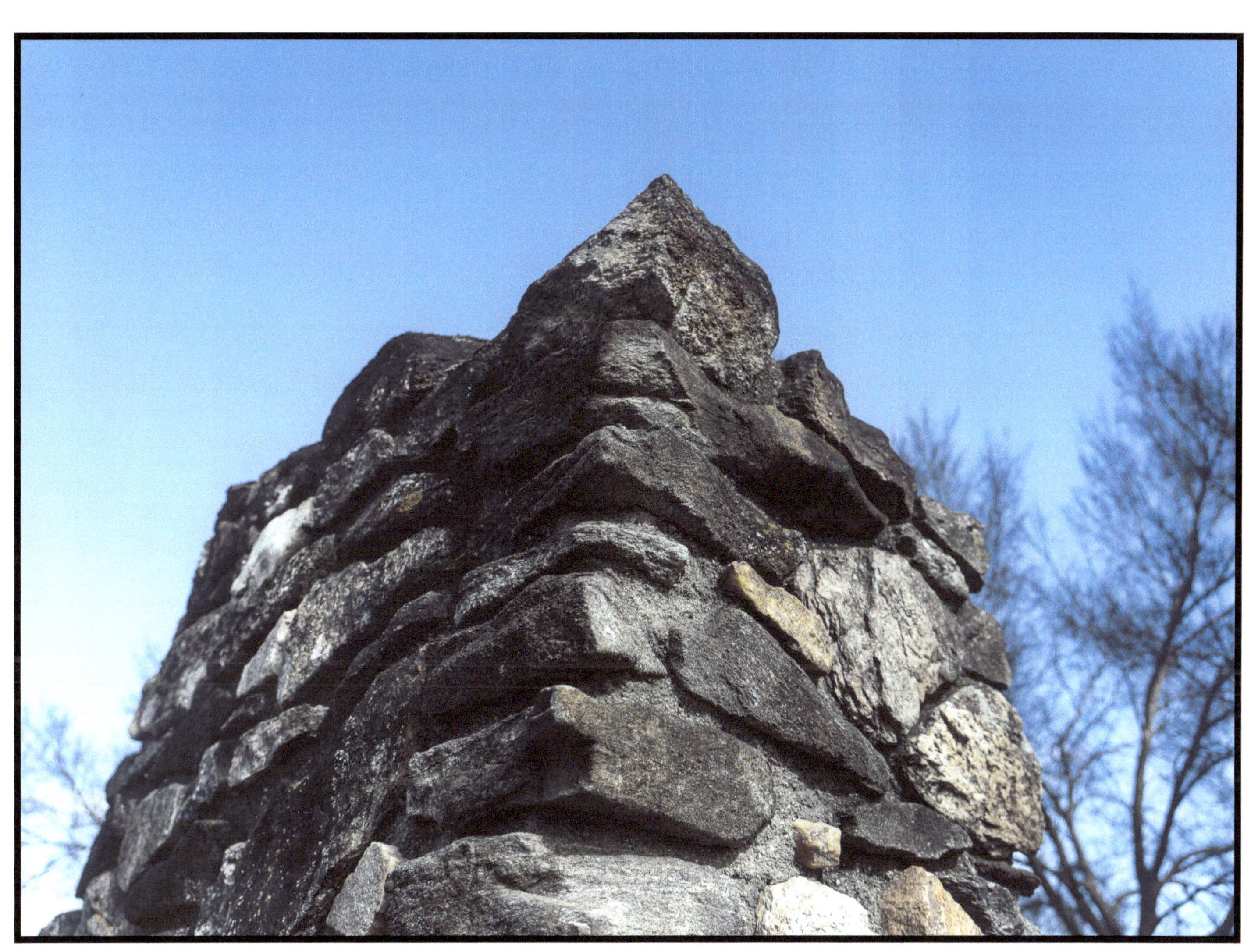

Rails

(Swain County, NC)

Every child should have one, a pair, really,
a matched set, set apart just the right width
so that one foot pressed against each one
leaves you stretched out about as far
as you can go, unable to move, feeling
almost trapped, almost actually in danger.

And every child should walk them as if
that's what they were intended for,
leading out of town, around the curve,
along the river, revealing the backsides
of people's homes, clotheslines and refuse,
the yards you weren't supposed to see.

And every child should learn to balance
atop the railhead without the constant
unsightly tipping from side to side,
should be able to step exactly the distance
between the ties consistently, almost
marching without kicking up ballast.

And every child should have a bridge
they go under to hide and look
at dirty magazines and smoke cigarettes
and place coins on the rails to flatten
and see if this could be the one
to cause the train to leap the tracks.

And every child should know the lonely
distant sound of late night travel
when bad dreams have kept them awake
wondering where they come from, what
they bring or take, and where when it's all
done they might return and call home.

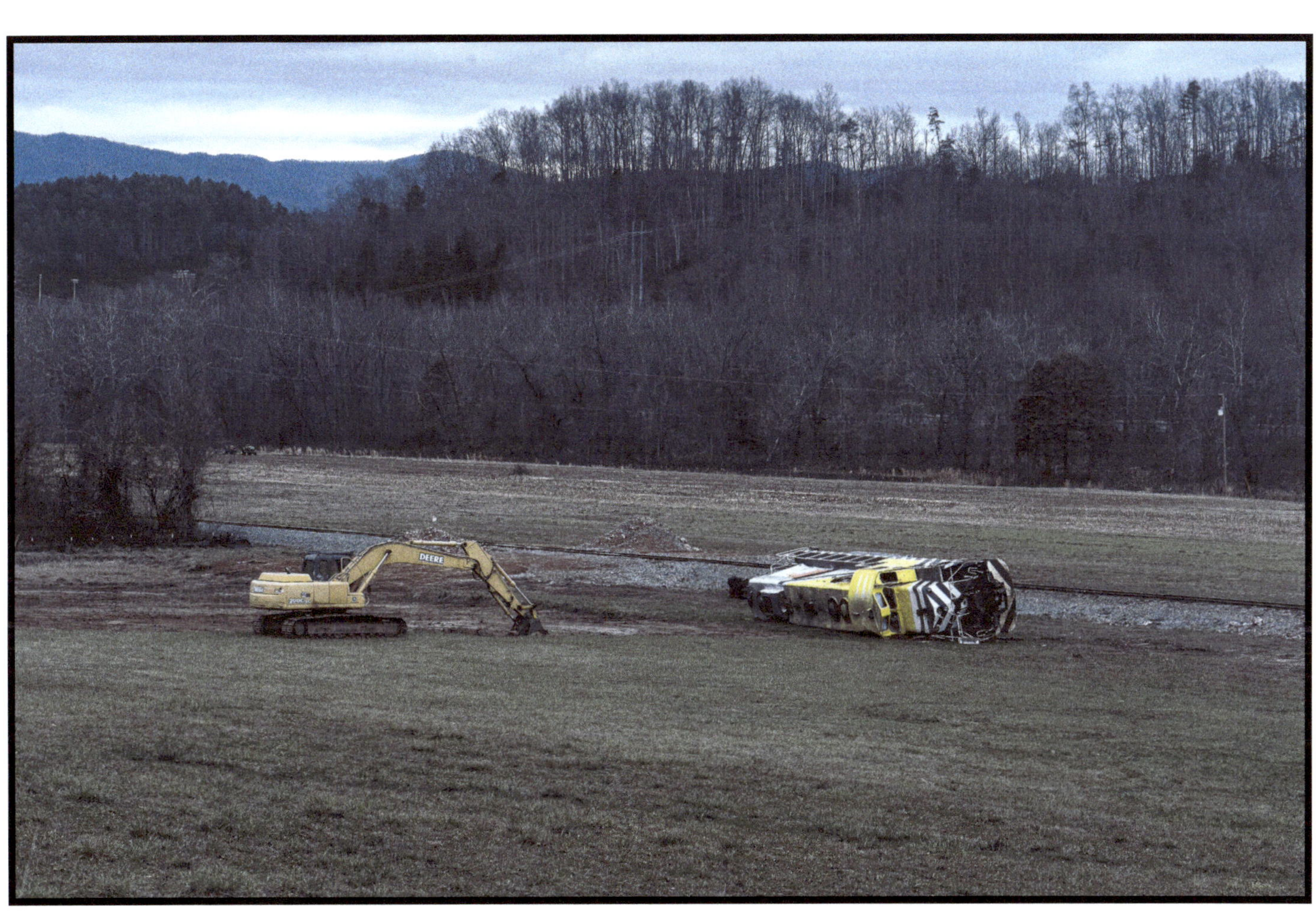
DEERE

Endowment
(Catawba County, NC)

He can't imagine what it used to be,
but having lived here 20 years he sees
the difference he's already made, stone walkway
leading to detached porch with seating and grill,
herb garden with rosemary, sage, thyme
well established, lasting through winters
regardless how cold, terraced field
leveled into backyard, euonymous
hedge, camelia, quince, forsythia,
bee balm, chrysanthemum, helleborus,
something blooming nearly every month
of the year, a grove of trees
in the back corner separating neighbors,
hawthorn, sycamore, cherry, as good as
any wall, and better loved,
and others scattered across the yard,
magnolia, pussy willow, maple,
pear, peach, plum, pecan,
a row of Nellie Stevens Hollies,
all grown to 30 feet or more.
He knows most of this will outlive
himself and he feels proud about it
knowing if nothing else will last
at least he'll have this to share as legacy.

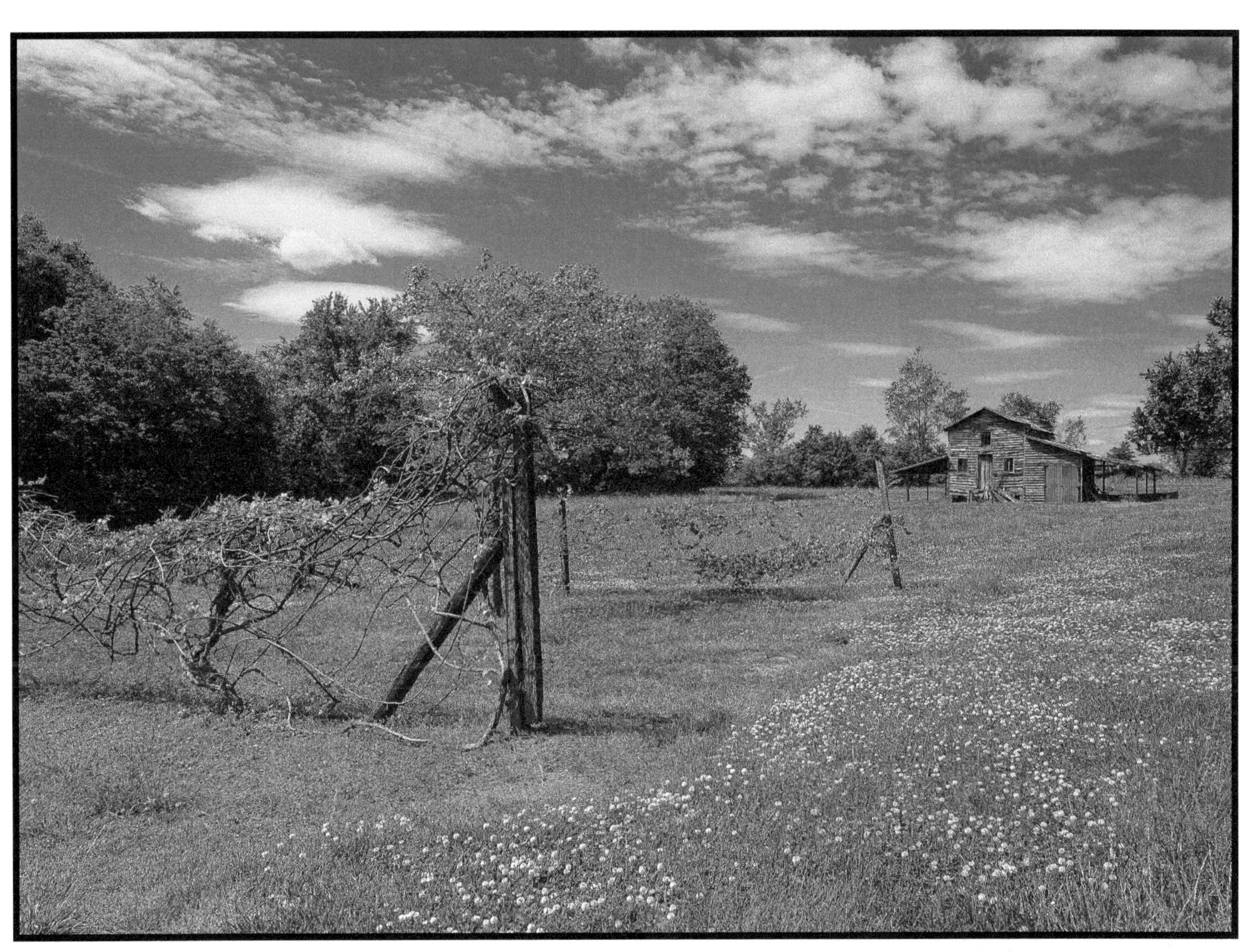

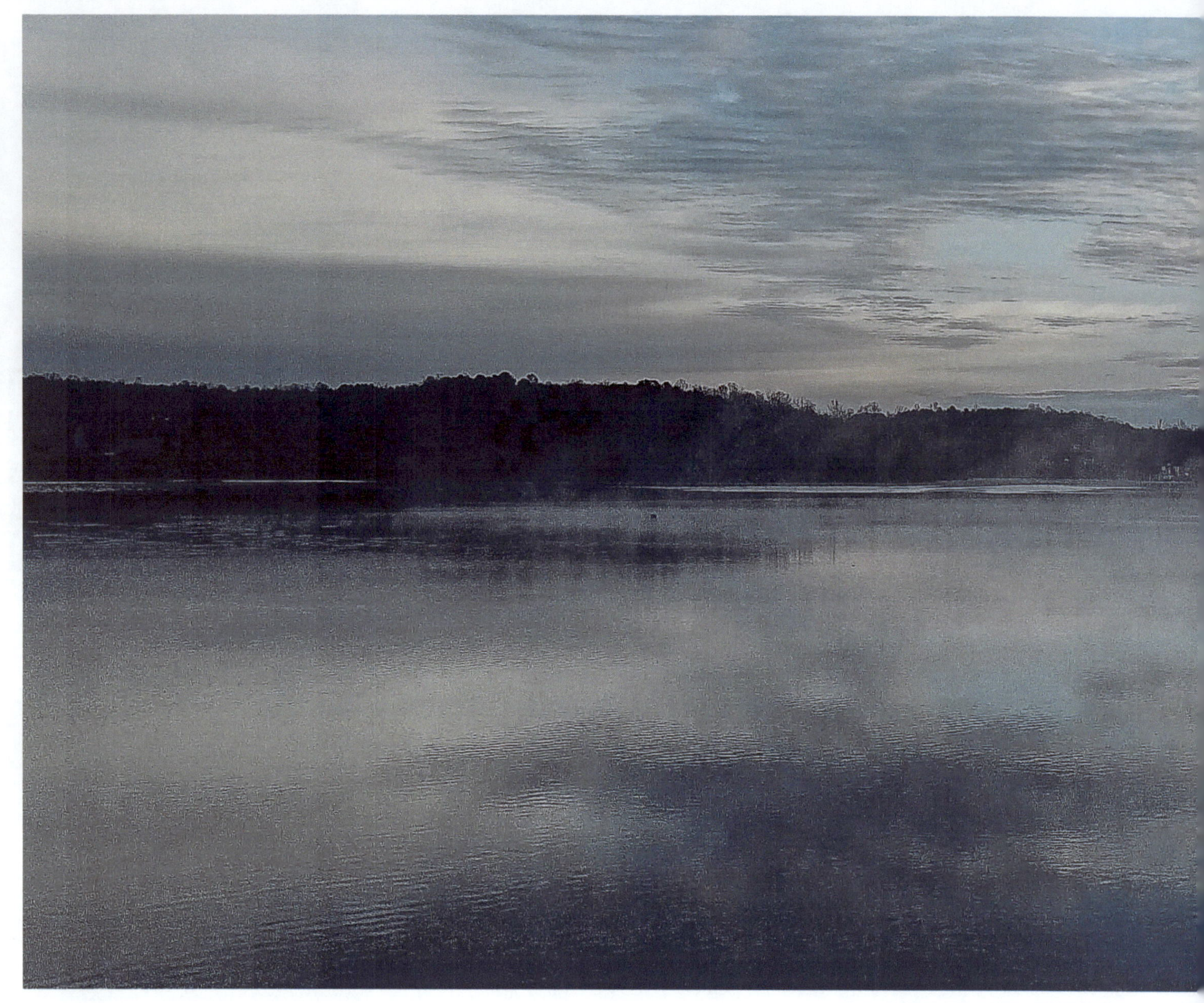

The Ontology of Rivers

(Catawba County, NC)

Like all rivers this one starts in a place,
in many places, without names,
every gorge, valley, and hollar
starting one, up past Silver and Steele,
Gunpowder and Crowders,
Dutchmans and Canoe,
even past Limekiln Creek,
Caney Branch, Muddy Branch,
Roaring Fork, Bee Rock Creek,
Thunderhole, springs and streams,
brooks and trickles, backyard washes,
gullies periodically filled with rain water,
scattered across NC mountains and foothills,
east of the Blue Ridge, running downhill,
from Mitchell and Grandfather,
Hawksbill and Evans Knob,
gathering from all around it as it descends,
becoming Linville River, Wilson Creek,
Johns River, and finally, here, where rivers
begin to come together, Catawba,
named after people named after the river,

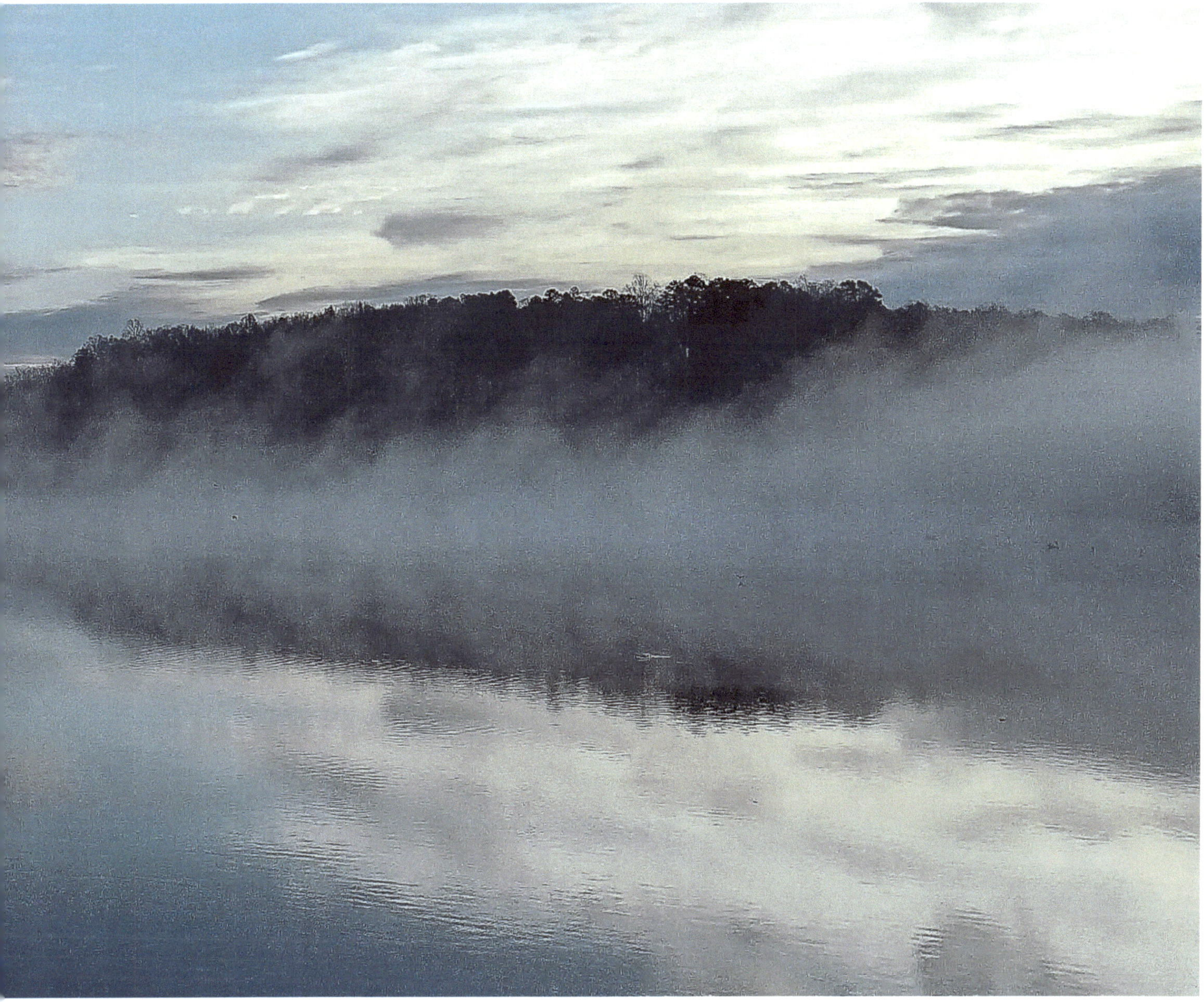

stopping only briefly behind dams
before continuing downstream, absorbing
other names, Henry and Jacob,
Irwin and McAlpine, Lyle and Allison,
Waxhaw and 12 Mile, until
even it changes to Wateree,
Santee, Cooper, and finds its way
all the way to Charleston Harbor
more than 500 miles in all,
to bring all it has left into the Atlantic.
And like all rivers this one,
older than names, older than lakes
and dams, older than cities and people
who live along it, is used for transportation,
hydration, irrigation, recreation, inspiration,
an endless array of teleological designs,
but the river itself intends none of this.
The ultimate existentialist, the river
simply is, and as long as there is rain,
and gravity, will simply continue to be.

yellow porch light
flickering in darkness
swirl of candle bats

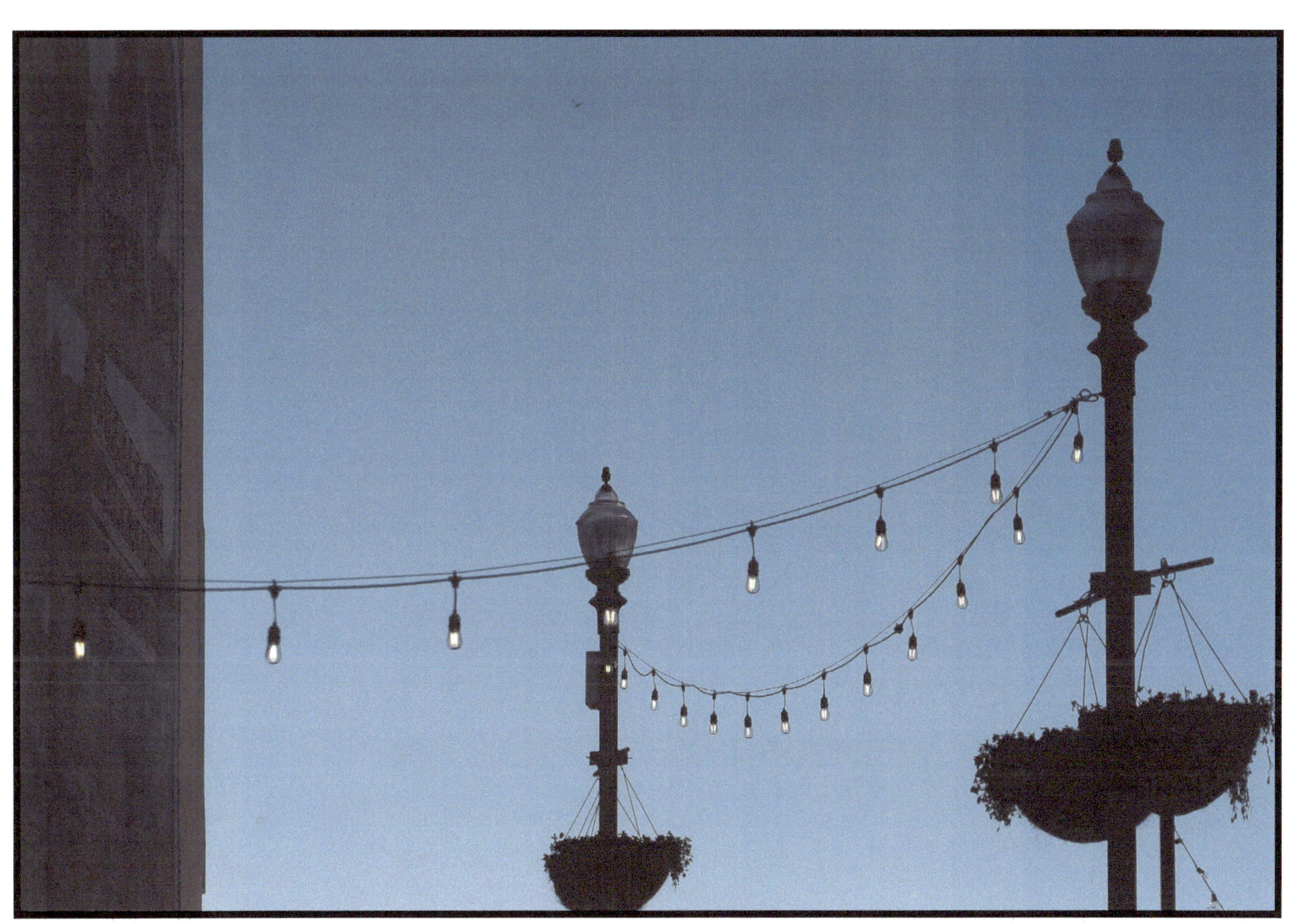

Midnight at the Good Old Days Café

(Catawba County, NC)

I said to my friend,
whose name might have been John,
but was probably Tim, or Ted, or Ron,
What is the past?
For I sometimes fear it.
Its shadow surrounds me night and day,
casting a face I cannot see in the mirror.

He nodded understandingly.

Is it the bud we grow out of,
the limbs we fly or fall from,
spent leaves discarded by trees
kicked up again in passing,
just a stack of yellowed papers,
headlines sure of their own importance,
pre-birth of this moment,
water broken on the floor,
residence of regret,
a shore we've swum out from
and can never get back to?

He smiled what might have been a smirk.
Is it soul, source, wound that never heals,
almost real fiction crafted by those who win,
fossil evidence of what might have been,
storied rings obscured by mere accumulation,
trunkless legs, boastful cities
built one on top of the other,
backward motion of a swing
essential to driving forward?

He sighed.

Is it a series of broken circles
beneath streetlights, a river
choked with sediment,
perfect for drowning in,
experience once removed for one
who remembers, twice for one
who listens, degrees of separation
multiplying exponentially
with the passage of time,
a window that won't open,
door that won't close?

He said, *Would you pass the goddamn*
ketchup?

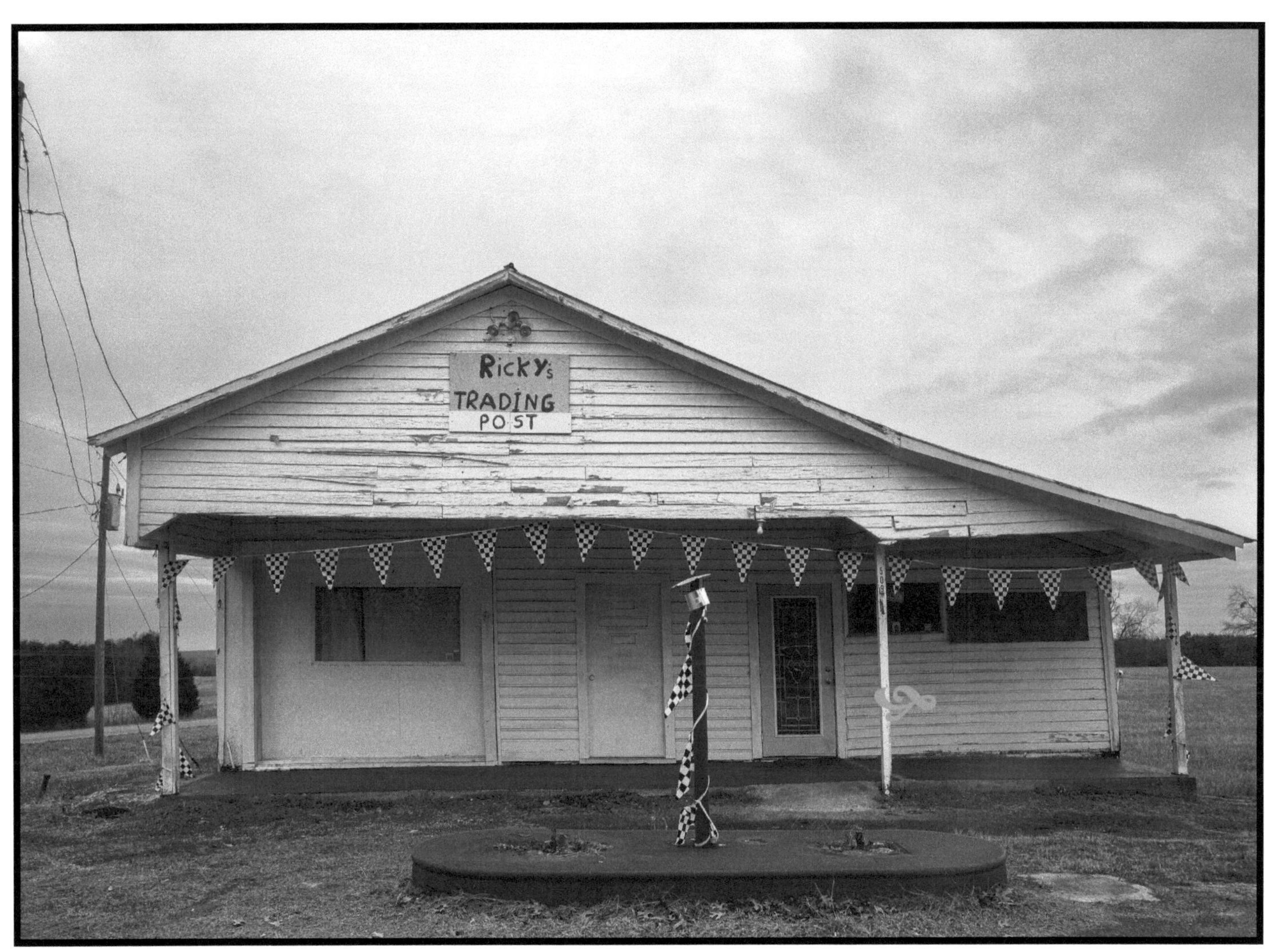
Ricky's
TRADING
POST

Apology

(Catawba County, NC)

He knew they'd all tell him
what he should have written about
and ask him why he left them out,
glorious things and inglorious,
people and places,
dead relatives and heroes.

Even in a place we think of as small
the list of things to write about
goes on forever: the Butterfly Girl,
Otter Out of Water, painted benches,
the Wheel of Time, the Speedway,
The Miracle of Hickory.

He'd want to say he was sorry,
that there would always be more,
and he could never find the words
to write about it all,
so he wrote this poem and put it at the end
hoping some might find it and be satisfied.

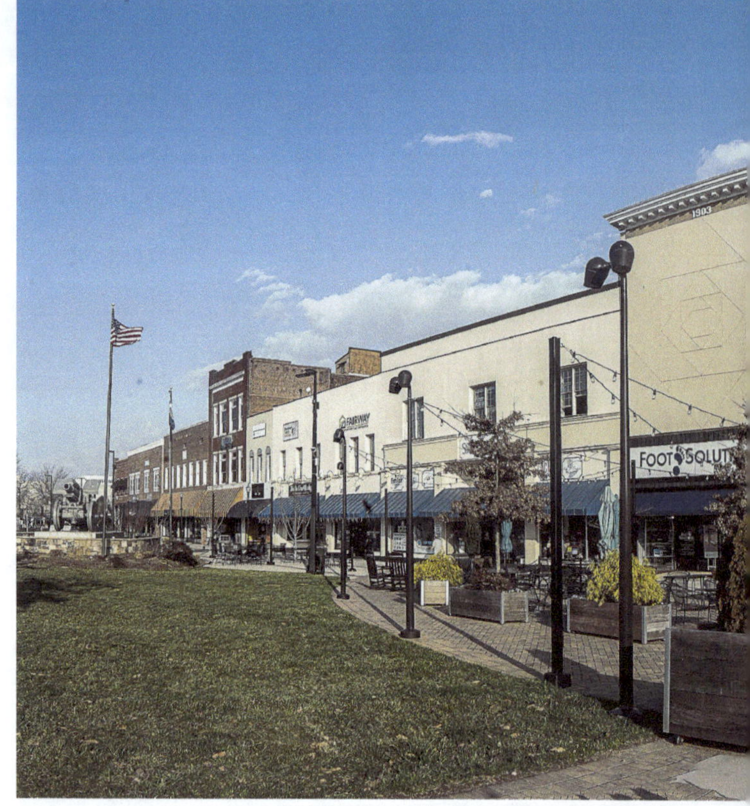

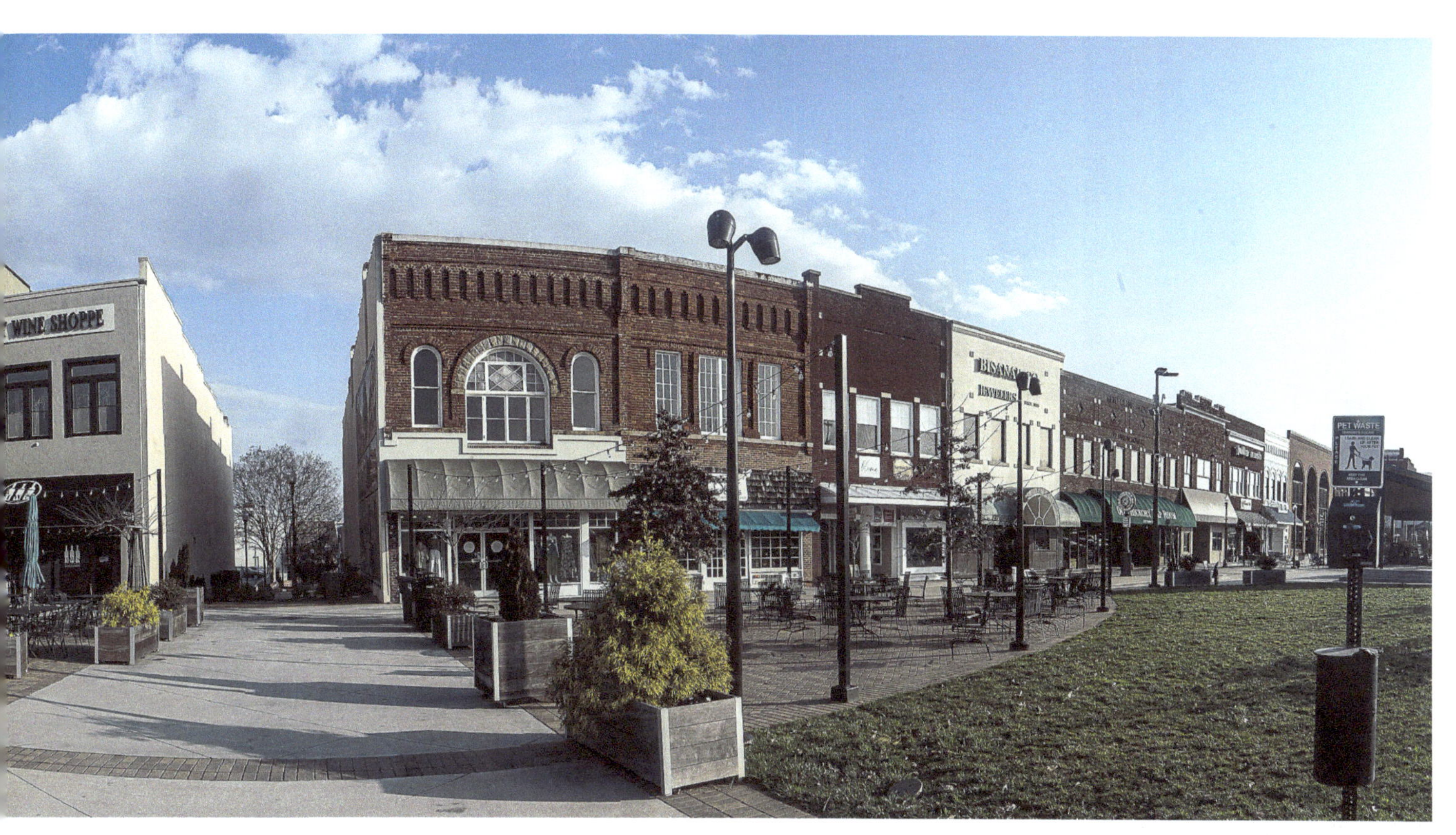
WINE SHOPPE
PET WASTE

ACKNOWLEDGMENTS

Grateful acknowledgment is due the following journals where some of these poems were previously published.

Dead Mule for "Existential," "Midnight in the Good Old Days Café," and "Rails"
Eunoia Review for "A Gift of Water"
Flutter for "Remembering Blue"
Iodine for "On Settlemyre Bridge"
Leaf Garden for "Open House"
Now and Then for "Appaloosa Landscape"
Outlook for "Keeper" and "Why So Many of Those Who Are Lost in Hickory Stay That Way Forever"
Poetry Pacific for "Looking for Faces in the Night Sky" and "Through"
Rusty Truck for [yellow porch light]
Strongverse for "Webwork"
Vox Poetica for "Art Appreciation" and "Reclamation"

"Coffee During Covid," [from this rocky perch], "Looking for Faces in the Night Sky," "Secrets of Southern Sweet Tea," "Through," [wildflowers blooming], [yellow porch light] were previously published in *Prepositional* (Redhawk, 2022)

"Cidada" was previously published in *Sky Full of Stars and Dreaming* (Redhawk, 2021)

"Address" and "Thinking About the Next Big Bang in the Galaxy at the Edge of Town" were previously published in *Thinking About the Next Big Bang in the Galaxy at the Edge of Town* (Main Street Rag, 2015)

"A Study of Steeples" and "Walking in Woods with Nowhere to Go" were previously published in *Country Roads* (2012)

The photo that accompanies "Mill Village" was previously published in *We See What We Want to See* (Redhawk, 2017). The photo that accompanies "Thinking about the Next Big Bang in the Galaxy at the Edge of Town" was published in *Thinking about the Next Big Bang in the Galaxy at the Edge of Town* (Main Street Rag, 2015). The photo that accompanies"Happy Valley" was published in *Country Roads* (2012)

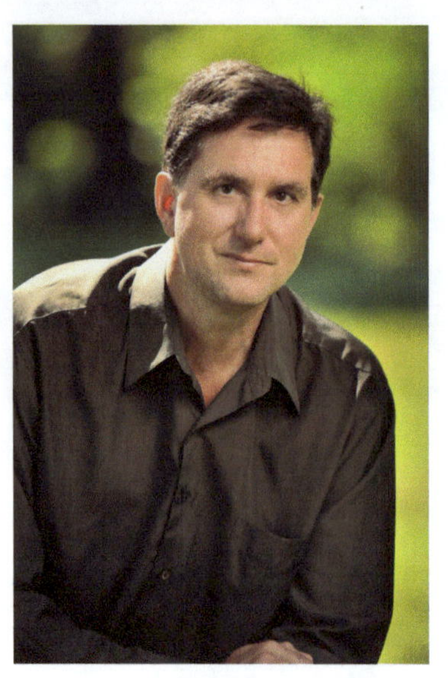

Scott Owens is the author of 20 collections of poetry and recipient of awards from the Academy of American Poets, the Pushcart Prize Anthology, the Next Generation/Indie Lit Awards, the NC Writers Network, the NC Poetry Society, and the Poetry Society of SC.

His poems have been featured on *The Writer's Almanac* eight times, and his articles about writing poetry have been used in *Poet's Market* four times. He has twice been nominated for the National Book Critics Circle Award and to be NC Poet Laureate.

Owens holds degrees from Ohio University, UNC Charlotte, and UNC Greensboro. He is Professor of Poetry at Lenoir-Rhyne University, and former editor of *Wild Goose Poetry Review* and *Southern Poetry Review*. He owns and operates Taste Full Beans Coffeehouse and Gallery and coordinates Poetry Hickory in Hickory, NC.

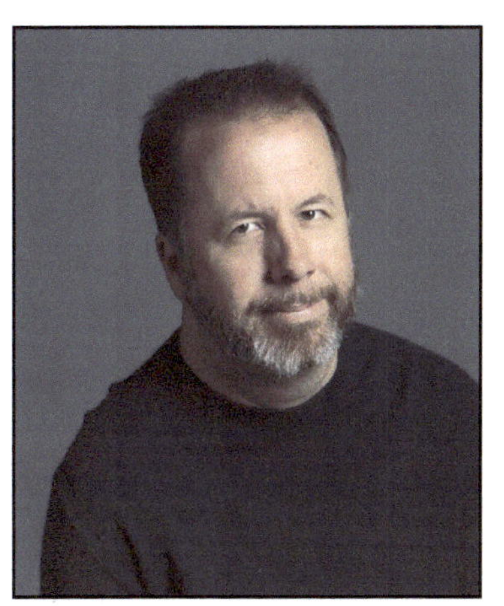

Clayton "Joe" Young is the author of 11 books and is an award-winning photographer with a background in photojournalism. Young's work has been exhibited throughout the United States in solo and juried exhibitions.

In 2014, Young earned the Certified Professional Photographers (CPP) designation from Professional Photographers of America

In May of 2015, Young earned a MFA in Photography from the Savannah College of Art and Design. He is the Director and Senior Professor for the Photographic Technology Program at Catawba Valley Community College in Hickory, NC. www.joeyoungphoto.com

www.ingramcontent.com/pod-product-compliance
Lightning Source LLC
LaVergne TN
LVHW070127110826
845147LV00002B/205

* 9 7 8 1 9 5 9 3 4 6 2 3 4 *